"Growing up and maturing into the human one aspires to be is not always black and white; sometimes vivid colors must be thrown into the mix to produce a masterpiece as Armani has truly done with his young life."

-Brandon Daniels

"This book is a quick read, but its impact on you as a reader will last a lifetime."

-Asher Jacobson

"This memoir is the first installment of a contemporary hero's journey, and it's a book that the world is starving for. While most of us are living constipated lives chained by imitation, Armani's soul came thundering out of the void with a flair for originality and embracing the extremes in life – plumbing the depths and soaring to the heights – and learning to love it all. This book serves as an energetic attunement that bathes the reader in the frequency of aliveness, inspiring them to sink their teeth into the marrow of their own lives, to commit fully to what's in front of them, to honor the practice of deep reflection, and to live uncaged, unhinged, and unapologetically in pursuit of one's dreams. Through the rawness of Armani's storytelling, you can expect your life force to be ignited and the spirit of 'Pounding Chest' to awaken within your own beating heart."

-Mica Schuchardt, ND

"Energetic, purposeful, entertaining and personable"

-Cristóbal González

"'Pounding Chest' is a story of renewal and perseverance. The author's "pro-matic" story-telling captures the reader's attention and forces you to root for him through the good and the bad. Antonellis invigorates passion for what he believes in and this idea is clearly depicted as he walks you through the hilarious and sometimes extremely serious moments of his life that have shaped him into who he is today. I am inspired to make meaningful changes in my own life and am excited for the future of this promising young writer as new adventures await him."

-Chase Silberbusch

"A personal account that will surely take your breath away. Exhilarating, fast paced, and emotional, Armani's journey will send forth feelings of inspiration and hope."

-Ian Tran

"To feel deeply, seize the moment, memento mori (remember your inevitable death) and take in all that life has to offer is invaluable. Armani captures those moments in his 20's which now gives him the perspective to carry forth through the rest of his life."

-Chris Matthews

POUNDING CHEST

Armani Antonellis

PC PUBLISHING

Published in Portland, Oregon

Identifiers:
Paperback ISBN 979-8-9876475-0-9
eBook ISBN 979-8-9876475-1-6
Library of Congress Control Number: 2023901821

1st edition 2023

A friend recently told me that confident, adventurous humans are bred through strong parenting. This book is for Mom and Dad. I'm eternally grateful to be your son.

A few names have been changed to protect the identity of those individuals.

Table of Contents

Chapter 1:
Game Time

Guy, Armani

My journey began in Poway, CA where I was born two days before Christmas. December 23, 1994, to be exact. I was fortunate to be raised by two amazing, love-filled individuals who were very supportive despite my crazy ventures. I grew up in Murrieta, California, a small town located half-way between Los Angeles and San Diego. At the time, it was considered a suburb but today it is overpopulated as families search for cheaper housing options in Southern California.

My father, Domenic, decided he wanted to be an electrician around 5 years old. He grew up humbly after his parents immigrated from Italy to Boston. They didn't have a lot of money but worked hard to provide for their children. My dad liked to play hockey, but didn't have the money to buy a hockey stick. He found a slab of wood and duct taped a clothes hanger to the end of it. His friends called him "The Clothes-Hanger". My Dad's ingenuity continues to this day, he is always taking spare pieces of junk and turning them into something useful. He's mostly an introverted guy who enjoys playing with computers and car engines.

My mother, Karis, grew up in Iowa in a small farming town. She grew up with four sisters and one brother. One of her sisters moved to Boston after high school, and my mom joined her. She met my Dad out there and they dated for many years before getting married. Before the wedding, my Dad's father, Antonio, died of colon cancer. He was a big part of the family. The stories I heard about Antonio stuck somewhere inside me. He reminded me of myself.

He was a stone mason by trade but had a variety of jobs including tending a bar, landscaping, and serving as a forest ranger. On the weekends he played bocci, an Italian game also known as lawn bowling. Antonio made his own wine, and loved kids. He even watched after his neighbor's garden. The deal was if he maintained the garden, he could share its harvest. At work he was called "do-by-eye". When everyone else pulled out a tape measure or ruler, Antonio would measure everything by eye. I really wish I had gotten to meet him. Sometimes I feel like his spirit is around, guiding me.

My mom was home with Guy (my brother, short for Gaetano) and I often as we were growing up. But she also had a number of career paths including kitchenware sales, nannying, and tutoring. Where my dad had the street smarts, my mom had the book smarts. She's exceptionally thoughtful and organized, which helped in running the household, and providing for my brother and I.

Growing up in the 2000s kids still played outside almost every day. Video games and Pokémon were entering pop culture. I remember one summer my mom made a deal with Guy and I. She said if we wanted to play one hour of Pokémon on our Gameboys, we had to first read a book for one hour. My mom is an insatiable reader, and I'm truly thankful to have picked up the habit of consistent reading from her.

..

During middle school I began having very vivid dreams while sleeping. I was able to induce myself into lucid dreaming. Lucid dreaming is equal parts frustrating, breathtaking, powerful, and fragile. You must have some sort of method to check your reality, kind of like the movie Inception. Once you realize you are in a dream, you are able to take control of it and literally anything you can imagine and believe can unfold before your eyes.

There are a few notable rules that come into play, for my experience at least. Sometimes, when I realized I was in a dream, I would become so excited for what was to come that the excitatory energy would raise my brain waves from the sleeping state to the waking state. Once I was awake, I could not return to the lucid dream. This was particularly frustrating.

Many times I would realize I was in a dream, become too excited, and wake up. The opportunity for deeper exploration was lost. But when I did keep my excitement contained, I would indulge in the quest to fly. I dreamt of walking through my childhood neighborhood, and usually would start by jumping. If I didn't believe with all my heart that I could graduate from jumping to flying, I returned to the ground. If I filled my heart with confidence and belief, I would soar all the way up through the clouds. It was one of the most exhilarating feelings I've ever felt. I would fly so fast I thought my stomach might eject from my mouth.

In hindsight, I believe these dreams were telling me I could do anything I imagined when I believed it with all my heart. The dreams also told me life wouldn't be easy, it wouldn't always work the way I wanted, and sometimes I'll feel like throwing up. Dream, and believe in your dream. Use everything within you that can fuel your belief. Telling myself over and over again that I could fly, and really meaning it, ended up in me flying.

I encountered this phenomenon over and over as I grew older. For example, we would be on the road a little late to sports practice. I prayed over and over that the traffic would give us a path so we would make it on time, and it always ended up being ok. Maybe not right on the dot, but certainly not too late. In my college years I told myself over and over again that I would make the ball in the beer pong cup, and really believed it. You best believe I was sinking cups.

- .... .. -. -.-

Murrieta Valley High School Water Polo and its culture played a huge role in my high school years, shaping me into the man I would become. Freshman year, getting 'pulled up' to varsity was one of the ultimate honors. One defining moment was in summer training. Coach asked my best friend, Chris, and I if we wanted to swim with the big boys. We knew the swimming would suck. We also knew that we were somewhat ready. We said yes. Saying yes to challenges continued to be ingrained within me for the rest of my life.

My brother's class was much larger than mine, and he was disappointed that he didn't get pulled up early. We both transferred away from our friends to a different high school to play on the winning team in the region. In addition to our busy practice schedule, we were introduced to a new world of advanced classes and high school girls. This laid the groundwork for a stressful internal environment. My brother took not getting 'pulled up' to heart. Occasionally, he would get into conflicts with classmates and teachers at school.

One day he ran away from home with the intent of no return. My mom came and told me, she was pretty shook. She had been trying to call him all afternoon (it was night) but he ignored every call. I took a deep breath and pulled up his number. He answered right away. He said that God would provide the path for him, and home isn't where he needed to be right now. He sounded fairly distressed. I told him that we all loved him and wished he was here, but if that's what he believes I'm not forcing him into anything. He called back 10 minutes later asking me to come pick him up. The energy coming off of him when he got in the truck with me and dad.... I've never experienced energy like that in my life. Raw. Carnal. Chaos. Fire. Life?

– .... . .–. . ..–. ––– .–. .

As high school continued, I generally had a great time. I dipped my toes into the thrill of the party, and quickly kicked it up a notch or four. It was a California spring day (off-season for water polo), and I had the SAT exam the next morning. One of my homies was throwing a house party, everyone had been talking about it all week. I remember sitting in my boys car splitting a bottle, and then an hour later I was absolutely sloshed. I had been texting my mom throughout the night about staying the night at a friend's house. She didn't like that idea. I was sitting on a bench in the backyard, where everyone was hanging out. Suddenly my mom walks around the corner. Everyone scurries away to unhidden corners of the backyard. One of my close friends stuck around to help me out.

My mom asks, "Armani, are you drunk?!"

To which I casually replied, "No, mom." And then proceed to stand up, take one step, and fall on my face. I was half carried to the car by my mother and friend. On the ride home she voiced her worries about the SAT. She felt she was getting drunk merely by smelling the reek of fermented pertater drifting out of my oral cavity. When we got to the house, my dad immediately provided a sense of comic relief, which I was thankful for. I was soon hunched over the toilet, my father laughing and carefully sticking bread in front of my face for me to eat and soak up the poisons.

The next morning my mom made me a breakfast burrito before rushing me to the test. About 16 minutes into the exam, I threw up on the ground next to my seat. All the girls turned around "you poor thing, I'm so sorry." I was still drunk and silently laughing hahaha. Sweating bullets, I walked myself outside and explained to the moderator there's no way I could finish this test.

Called my mom. She was not stoked. On the drive home, she proceeded to 'educate me' on how I would be homeless and working at McDonald's when I grew older. At the time, I exchanged unfriendly words with her. I felt like my soul was sprawled on the ground in a hungover mess. I was reaching a hand for help back onto my feet, but instead it was spat on and scolded.

As I matured, I realized that past traumas of my Mom and her family had been echoing in her subconscious, and the mama lion feared for her firstborn cub. She didn't want me to fall victim to the alcoholic tendencies present in our family's history. It was an act of protection, but the way she went about it hurt my pride and ego. It also left me hesitant to reveal to her the truth of my future intoxicated troubles.

When I walked into school on Monday, I was greeted with a standing ovation in the quad. All my friends had naturally heard the story, as stories get around in high school. They thought it was hilarious and epic. I drank up the attention like an elixir. It reassured me that I wasn't completely flushing my life potential down the toilet. It also started to create this identity within me, that I could be this kid who goes hard at the party. This identity was now associated with the positive reinforcement from my friends, despite my parents responding in a different fashion.

Mom and Dad sat me down and told me if I kept partying like this, they would no longer pay for my water polo. I decided water polo was definitely more important. I stayed out of trouble, and took the SAT in a sober state a few months later. I scored in the 97th percentile in the nation for the math section. McDonald's my ass.

··

Water polo players come out a different breed. Every year we had a tournament in Coronado, a small island near downtown San Diego. During the tournament, there were all kinds of United States Navy SEAL recruiters. The SEALs training is notoriously brutal, an absolute beast of physical challenges and military training. Water polo players were known to do well in SEAL training, since we're already used to getting clobbered and drowned on the daily.

One of my favorite things about high school water polo was the team yell before the game started. I still remember the first time I got to hop in on the varsity yell. We would all get into a huddle in the pool, with one of the captains leading the questions, and everyone else responding. It started with a few slow claps, which gradually became faster and louder before we erupted:

"What time is it?" "GAME TIME"
"What time is it?" "GAME TIME"
"What time is it?" "GAME TIME"
"What are we gonna do?" "WIN"
"What are we gonna do?" "WIN"
"Who are we??" "NIGHTHAWKS!!"

I was absolutely buzzing with energy jumping into the pool after that.

My junior year I was in a position to make a huge impact on our team. During summer prior to the season, my game was getting hot. I was stoked. Early in the season, however, I injured my shoulder messing around on a pool deck at my friend's house. I separated my throwing shoulder, which put me out for a few weeks. My hard-ass coach was anything but supportive during this injury.

During practices I would get in the pool and train my legs for hours. I remember one day we had a game which should have been a pretty easy win. Our opponents were local, and we knew most of the guys on their team, including their strengths and weaknesses. We also had never lost to them before.

A few hours before our games, Coach would have us get into the pool and do a light warmup, and run through a few drills to get our heads thinking about water polo. I didn't get in the water that day because I was still injured and wasn't playing in the game. We were playing an away game, at a pool we were familiar with. Around halftime we were not looking good. We were behind by 2 or 3 points. Coach had everyone doing pushups on the pool deck during our half time break. When everyone hopped back into the pool, he turned to me and asked how long I *wanted* to be sitting on the bench in my school clothes?

What the shit kind of a question is that?

I replied, "I'm injured, what do you want me to do?"

He later told us this story of a player he had who sawed off his own arm cast to be able to play in a title game. Coach said that was his favorite player. He liked the commitment and sacrifice. I thought he was psychotic.

After my recovery, Coach wouldn't even start me in the games. During summer I would have games leading our team in both goals and assists. Now I wasn't even starting. It definitely hit my pride, and my ego. I felt like he didn't actually care about his players, besides one or two favorites, and he really just cared about his team winning. My senior year I was in great shape but I didn't play that well. I would have my moments, but lacked consistency. My previous dreams of playing ball in the NCAA had faded away.

.— ——

Towards the end of high school, my dead-honest life goal was to go to San Diego State University and party my ass off in the frat life. I was waitlisted at San Diego State University, but decided to go to community college since they had a water polo team. I would also save my parents the more expensive investment at SDSU.

I had the opportunity to take a lifeguarding class my senior year. One of the instructors used to work as a beach lifeguard in San Diego. I thought that sounded fucking awesome. I would hang out with him and listen to his stories of rescues, pier jumps, surfing, sand and salt.

I signed up for the beach lifeguard academy, and drove out to the beach on the weekends for training. I absolutely loved it. We would show up on the beach at 8am for an early swim or run. We toured a different beach in San Diego each day. Everywhere from Imperial Beach on the border to the beautiful coves and kelp forests of La Jolla. Each beach provided some new scenery and a specific lifeguard skill training such as rescues with a surfboard, rescues off a pier, watching the water, or medical calls.

We would PT (physical training) once or twice per day. Every PT was ranked, and then there was a final ranking given out at the end of the academy. The higher rank you are, the more likely you will get picked up by a lifeguard agency for a summer job. It was old school, and it was fun. I started getting up at 6 in the morning before school to run a few miles. I had previously told myself that I HATED running. But once I got into shape and improved my time, it really wasn't so bad.

Senior prom was around this time, and my school was having it on the USS Midway in San Diego. That made it convenient for me, since I was already in San Diego for the weekends. The academy training the day of senior prom included an hours-long paddle on a rescue board. We could only wear shorts for our PTs. No wetsuit or rash guard. When you're on a board for that long, your nipples are the first thing to go. At the end of the day, I was BEAT UP. I limped into senior prom with bloody nipples. My date was a doll. She ended up driving me home a little early so I could get some rest before heading back to the academy the next morning.

After the academy, I went around to a handful of beaches to put in an application for my first job. Coronado was my top pick, I thought the island was absolutely beautiful and I had a great time there when we visited during the academy. I heard back from one or two beaches, but was still waiting for the phone call from Coronado.

One afternoon I got the call. I got the job! I was ecstatic! I jumped around the house hootin and hollerin. I landed my dream job!! One week after graduating high school, I packed my bags and moved my shit down to paradise, sunny San Diego.

team yell in the water

Chapter 2:
Operation Hustle

Michael McHan was my professor for Communications 101: Public Speaking. For some people, public speaking is an absolute nightmare. I kind of enjoyed it, despite that I passed out and pissed my pants while giving a speech in high school. Michael set such a laid-back vibe for the class, it was hard not to enjoy it. Let me tell you a bit about him. Michael used to be a professional dancer, he traveled Asia where he studied ancient knowledge with monks. He was an underwear model, and possibly the most jacked guy walking around campus.

He was in his mid-20s when I took his class, and shortly after he would become head of the communications department at SDSU. Michael could give you goosebumps, bring you to tears, make you love him or hate him with the power of his speech. He was an orator. And a fucking good one. He almost convinced me to change my major to communications. I can honestly say I learned more about myself and about life in that class than any other class I took in college.

He let us pick whatever we wanted for speech topics. I gave a speech explaining the day-to-day for a beach lifeguard. I started with "The first thing a lifeguard does at the beginning of the day... is lather up with sunscreen to prevent a burn." I then took off my shirt in front of the class and rubbed on some lotion. Michael loved it. My final speech was titled "How to cheat on a test and get away with it". I had hilarious pictures of kids going to extreme measures to glimpse the answer sheet on their neighbors desk. These early exposures to public speaking inspired me, and sparked a flame. I had a dream of one day giving a ted talk. I wouldn't pick this dream up again until years later.

——. .— —. ——. ... — . .—.

One day my roommate, Jared, told me his 'uncle' was coming down to visit for a few days. Cool, I thought. Little did I know this guy was one of the most bat-shit crazy individuals I would ever meet. Hustle, nicknamed for his love of hustling money, was running a giant weed operation in the mountains of Northern California. He apparently used to run strippers in Denver after he got out of prison. Hustle taught me a number of things not to do. Whining like a toddler when you don't get your way being one of them. He also taught me a few valuable lessons, for example, seize the day like it's your last. I have a few vivid memories of him.

One night Hustle, Jared, and I walked into the taco shop down the street after we had been ripping a bong all afternoon. He walks up to order his food. The first thing he asks the overweight Mexican cashier is "You know what I LOVE about cottonmouth? Getting my mouth all wet in some p***y." He gives her a big smile behind his low-fitted reading glasses and corny spiked hair.

I had a double-take... My guy WHAT??! The girl behind the counter laughed as he successfully got her phone number.

Another time he got a haircut, and the girl cutting his hair had her birthday the next day. Hustle kept telling her he was going to bring her the party. She was loving all the attention. The next day, Hustle had Jared and I walk in one at a time with "Happy Birthday" balloons, flowers, and cases of beer. He didn't even show his face. We were comparable to his henchmen, doing his dirty work. She already knew who it was from. This guy loved giving girls attention. Not always with the intention of something naughty, but he did give them the vibe that he was up to no good whatsoever. Hustle taught me how to talk to both women and men confidently, a skill that helped shape who I was to become.

One summer I went up to Hustle's weed operation in Northern California. He had around 200 weed plants on his property, cameras, rifles by the front door, the works. He told me if I paid him $1,000, I could fuck his wife. At the time he told me this, his wife and two kids were inside the house, almost within earshot.

The man was no doubt a hustler. The guy loved money. Maybe more than anything else in the world. He convinced me to start selling weed, and sometimes would throw a pound in my hands and tell me to pay him back once it was gone. I would usually sell most of it and smoke the rest. There were other times I had to pay some back out of my own pocket. It wasn't a situation I enjoyed being in, he could be a scary guy. I did, however, see the demand for weed in these young kids and how easy it was to make a little extra cash. Weed also brought people together, and it started to expand my social circles.

▬▬ ▪ ▬▪ ▬ ▪▬ ▪▬▪▪ ▪▪ ▬ ▬▪▬▬

At this time, I was working as a referee for high school water polo games. A pretty fun gig, but at times it was stressful. Especially when you have parents and coaches screaming at you. Officiating was a fun way to stay involved in the game and the community. Sometimes I would be working with legendary coaches in San Diego that trained Olympians in their youth. One day I had a game in North County San Diego. The only means of transportation I had was my motorcycle. I have to admit, I had smoked a bit of ganja earlier that day. As I was navigating towards the pool, I realized I missed a right, and needed to flip a U-turn. I was on a fairly empty, two lane road so I checked my mirror and saw a truck in the distance. I decided there was plenty of time. I slowed down and veered to the right, then leaned left to wrap the 180. Halfway through my turn I saw the truck suddenly extremely close to me. The horn blared at me, tires screeched. Bang. Nothing. Darkness...

Slowly, like a movie, 6 heads popped into my vision, all looking down at me with crazy looks in their eyes. I lifted my head to find my legs completely soaked in blood. An off-duty EMT calmly instructed me to relax and lie back down. An ambulance was on the way. Shit. My adrenaline was spiked so high, I barely felt any pain. The ambulance was taking me to Palomar. However, half-way through the ride Palomar conveniently lost the resources to see me, and my route was changed to Scripps Hospital instead. An extra 20-30 minutes. Also incredibly convenient, the medic on the bus failed to stick the intravenous line to administer drugs. I was getting low on liquids from losing blood, and had no immediate pain relief. Even more convenient, the adrenaline was winding down, and the pain kicked in. I was in agonizing pain until I arrived at the ER.

I remember giving my mom's phone number to someone, and being well cared for in the ER. Once the pain-killers kicked in I was able to finally breathe and relax. My left knee and left shoulder took the most damage from the accident. Since I had a padded bike jacket on my shoulder, it didn't get too scraped up. Most of the damage there hit my ligaments, tendons, and muscles. I was wearing thin white reffing pants, which didn't provide much cush. The truck left a gaping hole in the lateral side of my knee. Multiple fractures.

The doc talked me through his plan of care, then brought over a small hose to wash out the wound. I remember his finger going inside my knee hole and digging out chunks of gravel from the street. I couldn't feel anything, but I was sitting up with my eyes wide open in complete awe. This was crazy. A few hours later I was wrapped up in bed, in a private room. My parents walked in the door, and my mom immediately had tears in her eyes. Her baby boy escaped death. My helmet was savagely torn across the face shield. My dad handled the situation with more poise, but they were both awfully worried about me.

After 2-3 days in the hospital, I was ready to head home. I had 2 hairline fractures in my knee, and an AC (acromioclavicular) separation in my shoulder. Both shoulders were rocked and limited in their use. I could barely lift food to my mouth the first day. Since neither shoulder had much strength, I was unable to use a wheelchair. For a while my domain was the couch in my parents' living room. When I had to shit, my dad would lift me up and carry me to the toilet. God bless him. I was 19 years old and peeing in a cup for the first week.

The doctor informed me I could start moving again as 'pain tolerable'. If it hurts, back off. If it didn't, slowly engage. It sounded simple enough. One thing he didn't have in mind was the number and strength of painkillers he prescribed me. At the end of the first week, I was slowly putting weight onto my leg with the help of crutches. I was so stoked on how fast it seemed to be recovering. Soon my leg started to swell up, so badly that I passed out on the couch, losing consciousness. My parents called an ambulance and I was once again in the hospital less than 2 weeks after the initial crash.

After some diagnostic testing, it was determined there was a third hairline fracture in my knee. As a result I suffered from internal bleeding, which resulted in minimal blood flow to my brain, and the brief loss of consciousness. How the original doc thought his 'pain tolerable' treatment plan would be a success is still beyond me. Over the next couple months, I had frequent visits to rehab, watched all the Harry Potter and LOTR movies, organized a ton of Snoop Dogg, Dr. Dre, and Tupac in my music library, and observed my family coming in and out of the living room about their daily lives while I was couched up.

This whole fiasco fueled a mistrust in the conventional medical system. I felt like my injuries were not that complicated. I thought the doctors should have been able to safely guide me back to health. How did such straightforward injuries result in a second hospitalization? This mistrust would guide me later on to explore other realms of health and healing.

My recovery went fairly well. I ended up playing my second season of community college water polo, seven months after the accident. Community college ball was not horribly competitive, and that allowed me to step into a strong leadership role for my team. I was a dependable player in the game, showed up every day, worked hard, and challenged others to try their best. The invigorating team yells of my past fueled me to form creative new yells that inspired confidence and got my team fired the fuck up.

Growing up I took on some leadership roles in boy scouts and water polo. This time, however, it was a different team dynamic. A bunch of 19-21 year old hooligans. We were in need of direction and were beginning to understand that our fate was in our own hands.

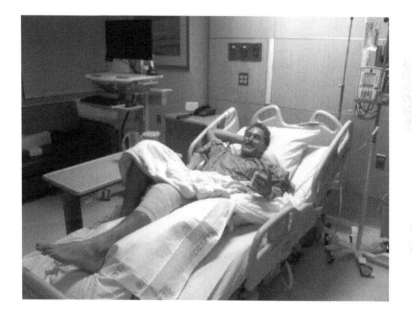

Chapter 3:
AZC Takeoff

After the accident, I moved into an apartment with some hometown friends, down the street from San Diego State University. Party. Fucking. Capital. I felt in my soul this would be one hell of a ride. Dreams of wild nights felt like they were within my grasp.

My studies were pretty shit while I was living there. I thought it would be cool to be a pilot. One advantage of community college was the opportunity to take a variety of classes. I signed up for a private pilot class, but the instructor wasn't very engaging. I felt like we were just repetitively doing the same flights over and over on the simulators. There certainly was no Top Gun action going on. Instead of going to class I thought it would be more fun to tip beers and play beer pong.

I remember going to a house party one weekend shortly after I moved near SDSU. Right when I walked in the door, some skinny chump walked up to me and said:

"Hey bro! You gotta rush this year!"

I said, "Why?"

"That's the only way you get real pussy around here!"

"Real pussy? Haha I'm good I can get that on my own bro. Good luck with that."

"Hey bro, you gotta rush!!" He said, putting his hands on me.

"Yo, get the fuck off me!" I shoved him back.

This stereotypical portrayal of the frat douchebag was presented to me early on. I knew it was a thing, but I didn't know it was that bad. That's the only way you're getting girls? Lol, ok bud. I decided, fuck all these other fraternities. I could make my own fraternity. I always had friends that were misfits, but we knew how to have a good time. I let the idea brew for a while.

I got so good at beer pong, my boy and I started calling ourselves "Team Clutch". One day my roommate, Joe turned to me and said:

"Armani, if we had a frat what would it be called?"

I thought about it for 2 seconds. "Alpha Zeta Clutch". And so, the frat was born.

••• • •— •—• —•—• ••••

The initiation for Alpha Zeta Clutch involved a great American challenge:

One bottle of liquor
30 beers
⅛ oz of weed
1 large pizza
100 piece puzzle

Teams were drafted by designated captains, and each step had to be completed before you move on to the next. Smoking weed ain't happening until all your beers are finished. You could, however, start preparing your joints or ordering pizza early. It was a bit strategic to draft your team with both drinkers and smokers.

I had been working on a logo for a while and decided to get tank tops made for everyone after the challenge was over.

The first AZC initiation

My dreams of being a frat star were just getting started. I was always a bit of an idealist growing up. I dreamed big, and was willing to put in the work and imbue the confidence for those dreams. Dream, and believe in your dream.

..-. --- .-.

After the pilot class turned out to be a bore, I signed up for an EMT class. Emergency Medical Technicians are trained for higher-quality life support in comparison to your average lifeguard. The class I signed up for was filled with mostly other lifeguards, including some of my friends and coworkers. It was also taught by a seasoned, well-known Lifeguard, Ed Vodrazka. Ed's passion for what he did certainly left a mark on me. He was able to take complex physiological concepts in the human body and describe them in simple terms. He also had some amazing lifeguard stories that kept the class fresh and entertaining.

I started to thoroughly enjoy this EMT class. I was even studying in my free time which is something I had done only on rare occasions in the past. There was a fair balance of book work and technical skills to master. The technical skills tend to be easier for lifeguards since they are used to working with their bodies.

The intricacies of the body's blood pressure regulating mechanisms could sometimes throw these guards for a spin, but I thought it was absolutely magical. I ended up crushing the EMT class, and decided to keep studying the human body. Ed had talked about his prior work as a nurse, and the fulfillment he experienced while working in hospitals. Nursing was ringing the bells of direction for me.

During our EMT class we had the opportunity to do one ride-along in an ambulance and one shift in an emergency room (ER). The ER left a significant impact on me. I was basically interning as an ER tech for the day, helping the nurses and docs take vital signs and checking in on patients.

In the first hour, there was an older lady that had gone into cardiac arrest, meaning she didn't have much time to live. I was on one side of the bed with a practitioner. He told me to hold her arm steady as he tried to insert an IV (IV stands for intravenous line, which shoots medication into the veins to help manage symptoms). Her body, however, was shaking so aggressively that I couldn't hold her arm stable enough for the IV to go in. Her time of death was less than a minute later.

I took a step back from the hospital bed. Deep breath. My mouth was probably half-way open and my eyes looking into the distance. The lady was "DNR" meaning do not resuscitate. She knew she was getting old and her time was passing. If she got to the point where her heart stopped beating, she had asked the medical staff to not do CPR. It certainly wasn't anyone's emergent medical error that had resulted in her passing. But I felt like I didn't give everything that I had within me towards holding her arm steady. I could have dreamed and believed with more strength.

I made a commitment. For the rest of my shift, I would give my absolute all. I saw so many medical conditions in that one shift. A stroke patient with one half of his face drooping south. A tension pneumothorax, similar to a collapsed lung. One man fileted his wrist open jumping over the fence at the Mexico-US border, and border patrol brought him into the ER. We needed a translator for that one.

By the end of the shift, I was filling out chart notes, which was a bit above my pay grade. But even more importantly, I found an environment where I was thriving. I fed off the energy in the ER. The constant interaction with beautiful people, and the miraculous ways the body functions, had me hooked.

After the EMT class, I decided to pursue more classes on the human body. I signed up for anatomy, physiology, chemistry, and biology. These core classes would lay the foundation for my future studies and understanding of the human body.

.. —.. . —. — .. — —.——

While I was playing water polo at community college, a guy named Tyler joined the team. It was pretty typical to have a few guys try out that have minimal water polo experience. Tyler could barely hold on to the ball, and his personality was noticeably out of the ordinary. But he also talked about things I hadn't heard before. He caught my attention.

He had training in martial arts and eastern meditation, and was studying acupuncture. I remember I caught mono around this time. I felt like walking death. My previously injured joints from the motorcycle accident felt awful. My knee was in so much pain, it could barely hold my weight. Tyler offered to bring me healthy fruits and do an acupuncture treatment. He introduced me to a modality of Traditional Chinese Medicine called moxibustion.

He explained to me that moxa is an herb which also goes by the name mugwort. It is usually used for injuries by burning the moxa and holding it close to the injury. This effectively promotes blood flow and provides heat therapy, as well as supports the energy systems (or qi, pronounced "chee") of Chinese Medicine. For a more aggressive treatment, you can burn the herb directly onto the skin.

My knee had really been killing me, so we took pinches of this weed-smelling herb and placed them all over my knee. Tyler sparked a lighter, and let the moxa burn all the way down to my skin. I felt a strange tingling sensation in my nerves. He told me that meant it was working, and that I should sleep well through the night. When I woke the next morning, I felt like a charged horse ready to sprint a mile. WTF. I continue to use moxibustion to this day for injury recovery and joint health.

Tyler used to tell me he didn't sleep at night. Instead, he would meditate for insane lengths of time. He was attempting the supernatural, hunting demons and vampires. I thought he was for sure a quack back in the day. But as I got older, I learned we are all from the same source of being and soul. We have a variety of experiences while we are in this lifetime. I wanted to understand his claims. What has he learned or experienced that led him to believe this was his reality? Is some of his reality also my reality?

.— —. —..

During this time I was given the honor of assistant coach for the men's water polo team at San Diego Mesa College.

Taking on a leadership role while playing ball for the team provided the "luck" that found its opportunity when a prior assistant coach stepped down from his position. I happily took the opportunity, and constructed what we called a "dry-land" training program for these young bucks. Dry-land training in water polo can be nominal for anything outside of the water, but is usually associated with the weight room. I used some of the yoga-inspired dynamic warmups the previous coach used, a few of his weight-lifting exercises, and a dash of my own favorite lifts that I found valuable in my time playing water polo.

We had a strong team that year. There was a real shot at the San Diego title, which we got close to but never attained while I was on the team. In addition to the dry-land training, I hopped in the pool to scrimmage and demonstrate skills during normal practice.

The head coach, Nathan Resch, had a laid-back bro vibe to him. He also checked in with everyone regularly to see how they were doing. He is an absolute gem of a human being. I remember him having a talk with me towards the beginning of the season.

"Armani, I know that you are good friends with some of these guys. Your position on the team is different now, and you can't be partying with them as if you were their teammate."

I agreed with him, I couldn't be shitting where I was eating. This was a job, and a responsibility.

.— —.—. —.—. . .——. — .— —. —.—. .

While I was coaching, I continued to party with the guys. Against Resch's wishes. I couldn't help it. We were all the same age, and as we continued to spend time together in the pool, we also spent time together out of the pool. The season ended really strong, we took home the title in San Diego. I threw a rager at my apartment that night. We threw our arms around each other and sang Queen's "We are the Champions" at the top of our lungs.

A week later the girls water polo team was going to the state finals. They were really really good that year. We wanted to go support, and Resch offered to drive us in the bus. The boys were texting in the group chat. The bus ride sounded perfect. We could all drink at the game while Resch drove.

At the pool we had matching cheap flasks that we brought into the bathroom to fill with mixers. There were some parents in the bathroom that saw what we were doing, and they didn't seem to approve. As the games went on and the flasks grew lighter, we grew excessively rowdy. One of the parents from the bathroom told a pool manager that we had been drinking. We ended up getting kicked out of the pool for genuine drunken behavior. The girls final game hadn't even started yet.

I went down the exact route that Resch and I had discussed not to. Even worse, I had taken the party curriculars onto the pool deck.

The ride home was long and quiet. I was the last person to be dropped off by Resch. He expressed his disappointment. I felt like I let him down. I know he really valued having me around the pool.

"Armani, what happened man... We had such a good thing going. I loved having you on the pool deck, but you did the exact thing we talked about staying away from."

"I know, coach. I'm sorry. I did do the exact thing we agreed not to. It's hard for me to say no to social activities."

I realized I would no longer be coaching with Resch. I didn't realize I was walking away from more than a job. More than a way to pay the bills. I was walking away from fertile grounds for a deep mentoring relationship with Resch. He was the first mentor I grew close to. He was someone that really believed in me.

Chapter 4:
Coronado Beach

On the beach I had one particular weekend that was spectacular. While I was cruising through the sand in the Polaris ranger, I heard through the radio that a beach patron was unconscious and being dragged out of the water. Your boy sped a half mile towards the location and sprinted on foot to the scene. CPR was in progress. I immediately hopped in to help, taking over compressions.

A dead body was flailing beneath my arms, foam spurted out of the mouth and eyes rolled back into the man's head. He was middle aged and overweight. In lifeguarding, during a serious medical situation the main goal is to keep the patient alive and get them to the ambulance as quickly as possible. I was soon in the back of another ranger (about 4 feet long) holding a backboard with a dying man (about 7 feet long). I used my foot to keep him from falling off the back. The sand was nowhere near a smooth ride. We were bouncing around during the minute long speed to the medics. I did my best to continue compressions.

When we turned him over to the medics, they agreed it was too late to save him, but they assured us they would continue the optimal care standard and do everything they could. I was humbly surprised at my performance under the pressure and adrenaline rush at hand. My EMT training had paid off.

Radios in lifeguarding were a fun thing. We operated on the same frequency, and with the same codes, as the police and fire departments. Later the same day, another wild call came through my radio.

"5150 near tower 3."

5150 was code for a crazy person. A man was running down the beach starting fights with people. Once again, I found myself spitting a dust storm behind me as I slammed the pedal towards the latest event of the day. My sergeant, Evan, a small Asian man, arrived at the same time.

My primal instinct was firing up, telling me to rush the crazy person (5150 in radio slang) and take him to the ground. Evan had a different plan. He ordered me to care for a girl, the man's latest victim, who was screaming that he had shoved his fingers in her pussy. What the actual fuck was going on. I moved to calm down the girl, then turned to check on Evan. He already had the crazy man in an arm bar on the sand. Evan was about half this man's size. I took a deep breath and held my position, assuring the girl she would be okay. Police were on their way.

- - -

Most of the time on the beach was spent watching the water. Big surf wasn't very common in Coronado, and the water was only full with people in the middle of the summer. But during a hot summer weekend with big surf, we were making rescues all damn day.

One busy summer day a boy around 8 years old was getting caught in a rip current. A rip current is a body of water that accumulates after a big set of waves. After it accumulates, it shoots past the surf, returning to deeper water. We called these flash rips, since they can flash up really quickly. The surf was about 5-7 feet that day, and the boy was struggling to keep his feet on the bottom. Meaning, he was being pulled into deep water.

I ran out to him and clipped him into my rescue buoy to make sure he stayed afloat. As I turned around and gave an all clear sign to the other guards, we got slammed by a wave. The kid was ripped out of the rescue buoy, and I tumbled through the white water, not able to see what was in front of me. I reached out my hand and happened to grab his ankle just in time. I pulled him in close to me and kicked under and around the tumbling wave before coming back to the surface. The boy gasped for air.

"You're doing great buddy! Take a deep breath, we have to go under another wave!"

He took a dramatic gasp as if it's his last breath on Earth. I kicked under the water, and when we resurfaced, the waves pushed us back into shore. His mom and sister were on the sand waiting for us. They were both worried and grateful that he was alright. That rescue will always remain vivid in my memory. I'm not sure what would have happened if I didn't reach his ankle.

--- -. .

That year was truly a highlight in my life. Work was rewarding. My classes kept me engaged. The fraternity was thriving. I was in a romantic honeymoon of falling in love. I met a girl, Carley, and we clicked instantly. We became good friends before I made a romantic move. One night we were at a party and I convinced her to skinny-dip in the pool with me. We got kicked out of the party when the hosts realized we were hooking up in their pool.

I found a group of friends that I got along with really well, and was becoming a more outgoing, confident person. I felt spiritually more connected to people around me than ever before.

Spring break in San Diego comes to life 30 minutes south of the Mexico border. The beach town of Rosarito had the most poppin beach club on the west coast, Papas and Beer. "Papas" looks like a movie scene. It's decked out with massive pool parties, wet t-shirt contests, belly flop contests, and lots of tequila.

My first impression at the bar: the insane number of women's undergarments hanging from the ceiling. Naturally, all the girls I was with ripped their panties off and tossed them into the collection. A blurry night of body shots off of strippers and cigarette burns on my forearm ensued. In the morning, I woke up with the sun for a run-swim-run on the beach and meditated to set myself for the day.

I used to party so much I would not be able to get up for work the next morning. This happened many times, and cost me a few jobs. And depending on what I got into, my hangovers could vary a lot. One morning I got up and went for a run on the boardwalk. A homie threw me a beer after he saw me sending pushups and situps on the sand. I spun over a small wall, caught the beer, chugged, pointed to the sky, and continued to sprint down the sunny beach before jumping in the water to catch a wave or two. Hoots and hollers were screaming behind me. Testosterone fully firing.

"My hip hurts from trying to jump the bonfire last night. My head hurts from drinking and is still scratched from blacking out. My knuckle is also cut and infected from blacking out. My foot is scraped up from the bonfire. My elbow and knee are banged up from skating one morning. I really need to take it a little easier. No more wild shit like that for a while."

My weekend nights included mobbing to 6 different house parties or throwing my own at the crib. I would be in contact with 30-40 people minimum to see what was poppin for the night. It was thrilling. I was not the same shy video-game nerd I embodied in my youth.

•— — •• — ••••

About every other week while I was running AZC, I walked into a grocery store, loaded my cart with three 30 racks of beer, then turned around and walked out the door. No payment. Supplying my own parties with tons of free beer was great. You know what fucking sucks? Getting caught. I continued this nerve-racking feat for over a year until it happened.

I was almost back to my car when two undercovers rushed me, cuffed me, then walked me to the break room in the back of the grocery store. I had to wait a few hours for the police officer. I knocked out some squats and lunges in the handcuffs. The officer wrote me up for petty theft. When he finally let me go, I went down the street and spent 40$ at the liquor store to legally supply the party I was throwing.

"Oftentimes rules are guidelines. This mentality provided me with opportunities others would call lucky. It also got me into trouble on numerous occasions. Overall, I made an attempt to not do too much harm to anyone around me, and at the same time continue to spice up my life so it was more colorful and interesting."

"When I have kids they're gonna be badass mofuckers. Like I'll teach them moral values but I want them to want life so much, and to get after it with their head held high. Keep your mind sharp, and always be kind to others but hustle your shit and work the system at all times."

— •••• •

Heading into finals one week I got hammered 6 days in a row. I took adderall once or twice during the week to study. The morning after one particularly long night of jungle juice at my neighbor's apartment, I had an Anatomy lab final. The test started at 9 AM sharp. I woke up in bed at 8:30. I immediately sprinted to my car, flew down the freeway a few exits to campus, then sprinted almost a mile through campus. Some of my homies from the night before saw me and were hootin and hollerin. I made it to class one minute late. I heeled over, trying to catch my breath. My instructor laughed and handed me the exam. I was sweating... vodka. Vodka was leaking out of my pores. Fucking jungle juice. I struggled to stand up straight as I took the exam. I was still wasted.

I managed to pull off a strong A. My hard work during the semester paid off. I went home, worked out, then got ready to party once again. I literally had this tradition of getting absolutely hammered the night before each exam. I told myself it cooled my nerves off. I told myself I worked hard enough during the semester. At the time my stubborn ass either didn't understand or didn't care that I wasn't reaching for my full potential. Somehow it still worked.

·— —· — · ·—·

In the summer of 2016, I picked up an extra lifeguarding job to save money and go on a trip to Italy. I was working 7 days a week most of the summer. My new employer was the city of San Diego. A much bigger agency than Coronado. They had their first-year (rookie) guards stationed in Mission Bay. It was much less glamorous than working on the beach, but it was a good entry point into lifeguarding. Since I had some experience under my belt, and performed well in the PT's, I was in good standing to get "pulled up" to the beach sooner than my fellow rookie guards.

"Blacked out again. This time I didn't get up for work at my new job. I said fuck it, ordered a pizza, and then my boy hit me up about going to a day fade. I said fuck, yes! Had a great time there, called my sergeant back around 7pm apologizing for not coming in. A few days later I get a call back from him saying I'm being pulled up from the bay to my first beach shift. What the fuck."

I was stationed in beautiful La Jolla for the city of San Diego. Most of my days were spent on a locals-known beach, where there were less tourists and poor swimmers. The guards rotated between the tower, surf board, and ATV all day. What a great job. One of the most breathtaking experiences I had while guarding here is still firmly inscribed in my memory: I was driving down Scripps pier in La Jolla, about 50 feet over the water. The ATV throttle is ripped all the way open. The glowing sun was setting over the water, creating a sky of deep red and orange. The wind was rushing into my face. As I looked below me, a surfer was dropping into his last wave of the evening, a slow left.

View from the La Jolla lifeguard tower

Another thing I found to be mad fun: off-duty rescues. When the surf was good, I would throw on my pink boardies and whomp (body-surf) in the waves after I clocked out. When the guards were running in for rescues, I could spring over, help a few people get back on the sand, then dive back into the water to get pitted again. What a life.

Chasing parties and overindulging in substances was catching up to me. I got fired from my new job. My captain at my original job sat me down to have a talk. He knew I'd been partying too much. And I had been. I black out, get in a fight. Carley blacks out, gets in a fight. I have to pull a girl off her in the hallway and sit her ass back down at home and tell her to keep her hands to herself. I throw another rager, someone else gets in a fight, tables broken, the place is a mess. This is the point when I realized my drinking was getting excessive. It was starting to affect other areas of my life. Some nights I was putting down three 4 locos.

-    -   -

Before I took off for Italy, I spent some time at home. I had a talk with my brother when he came home from college for Christmas. He was saying some pretty twisted things about not needing other people around him. I tried to assure him that I have pre-judged people many times, but as I got to understand them we were able to form relationships that brought me joy, happiness, and perspective. I told him we need people around us in our life, we can't and should not try to take on all life's challenges on our own.

He expressed that he felt very differently. People around him were slowing him down, and he felt that he continuously needed space, to the point where he was constantly pushing people away. I was worried for him, given his emotional swings of the past. Guy was just lying on his bed, glaring at the ceiling with tears streaming down his face. He didn't even want to come home from school for Christmas that year. At the end of our talk, he refused to give me a hug.

My brother and I were on different ends of the sociability spectrum. I was saying yes very often, which was fun and spontaneous. But it also led me to morally-questionable activities. Guy was saying no often. The school he was attending operated military-style. He sacrificed his free time to graduate early and made long term goals a priority.

You hear things growing up, like "The people you go out to the bars with or get drunk with on the weekends are not really your friends." Or, "I bet in 5-10 years you won't actually talk to any of these people. You're just creating memories in a drunk, ingenuine haze." Well, I'm writing this book 6 years later and I certainly still talk to my friends that I was getting drunk with. And, more than that, I've moved to two new cities. I haven't lived in San Diego for 3 years, but I still talk to those same knuckleheads that stuck with me through the drunk trenches of my early-20s.

Chapter 5:
Europe

I saved up enough money and it was time to take off to Italy. I was going to see the motherland. I asked Carley to come with me on the trip. We planned to spend a few days in Boston with my cousin, then fly to Rome, tour around Italy, head to Paris, Barcelona, then back to Italy before heading home.

For a week we stayed with my aunt and uncle in a small town where my grandparents grew up. San Donato Val di Comino. My aunt was the only person in town who spoke English. My afternoons were spent with my uncle, learning the beautiful Italian language. Having my aunt around to help translate was especially helpful.

My father's mother, Nonni, passed away the previous year in Boston. She had a series of strokes that left her in and out of the hospital. She was the first family member to die who I had meaningful memories with. Nonni loved caring for my brother and me. We used to get packages in the mail with home-made sausages and, my favorite, "gazalunes". I was told this translated to "moon-cheese" but I'm still not sure how. They were baked pockets filled with cheeses and spices. Savory with the smallest kick. Being in Italy brought back memories I had with her. She was a classic Italian grandmother. The second your food was finished on the plate she would say "Oh, you like it? Good, I'll bring more." If you didn't finish your plate, she said "What's the matter? You don't like the food?" It was an inevitable spiral into a food coma.

Zia and Zio (Aunt and Uncle) showed me the house where Nonni grew up. I was told she shit next to the cows, and one year for a sweet Christmas gift, she was given an apple. World War II hit Italy much differently than America. Nonni saw her brother get blown up by a hand grenade in the yard when she was just a child. I saw the house where my grandfather, Antonio, grew up as well. Seeing my family's history, my roots, meant a lot to me.

● ●●●●▬ ● ●▬● ▬●▬▬ ▬ ●●●● ●● ▬● ▬▬●

Carley and I headed to the Amalfi coast for a day trip. It was a train and bus ride away from Zia Loreta's house. We spent most of our time in Positano, a small beach town with colorful houses decorating the side of a mountain. It was absolutely gorgeous. We enjoyed ourselves quite a bit. So much so, that when we were ready to leave, we discovered the last bus had already left for the night. We would have to spend the night in Positano.

Positano

Every. Single. Hotel. In. Positano was sold out for the night. We went to a local bar to drink and think about it. As it usually goes at a bar, we started making friends, and a kind older gentleman offered to let us stay the night at his place. It was our best option yet.

When we get to this man's house, the place is covered in puppets. Like, every square foot of wall space is a straight puppet-fest. Carley and I looked at each other with wide eyes. What the shit did we get ourselves into. The man explained that he loved making children's toys, puppets especially, and playing with them in the parks and giving them away to the kids...

I didn't sleep much that night. Puppet number 57 and 341 were giving me weird looks. We left early to escape a morning encounter with the puppet man and got back to Loreta's safe and sound.

.... .— .——. .——. . —. ...

Carley and I had a lot of down time together. We made some great memories, but we also drank a lot, and were fighting constantly. I've always been a big dreamer, an optimist, and even an idealist at times. I had dreams of working in healthcare, and had a strong belief in my dream. Carley was still trying to find her dreams, and her belief in her dreams. I think she started comparing herself to me, and it made her anxious about what she was doing with her life. Instead of enjoying the vacation, she was stressing over whether she was living out her purpose. Maybe the timing of the trip was right in my life, but not in hers.

One night in particular we went to a show in Venice. Carley was so drunk she was spilling drinks all over both of us. I tried to grab the drink to prevent further spillage, and she didn't like that. She yanked her arm back, and my shirt got soaked. She then proceeded to tell the bartender I was an asshole. The bartender looked at me understandingly and asked that I get her home safe.

The next morning I woke up before Carley and took a stroll through the streets and canals of Venice. It felt refreshing and freeing to have some alone time. I felt that I was giving all I could in terms of patience and understanding with her. When I returned to the hotel, I told her I couldn't do it any more.

We undoubtedly had great chemistry and similar interests. But I felt like we both needed to discover ourselves more as individuals before we pursued our serious relationship. She was devastated. I felt horrible. I just couldn't do it any more. Our lives were more valuable than a constant toilet bowl spin of emotions, draining into disrespect and embarrassment.

I acknowledged we both saved money for the trip, and told her she could keep traveling if she wanted to. I just didn't want to see her anymore. She flew back to California the next day.

..-. --- .-.

The day after Carley flew back I received an email from SDSU admissions. I applied to transfer into their Nursing program. I was really looking forward to a more formal, focused education. I didn't get in.

The following week in Paris I was a hot mess. For the first time in my life I was alone in a foreign country and knew nobody around me. My heart wounds were fresh from the breakup. I called everyone close to me and got drunk at the bar. I called Carley, who actually picked up and said she missed me. I even bought a plane ticket back to California. I was emotionally torn and rationally dismantled.

I woke up the next morning and canceled my flight. I was certain this breakup happened for a reason, and things were not going to be easy. I decided to finish my travels, try to enjoy myself, then head home when I had my fill. I stayed in bed for hours and watched YouTube videos from my favorite influencers; on recovering from a breakup. Eventually I took a normal breath without tearing up and attempted to stand up with my head held high.

Paris was especially rainy and I didn't get to do much. A few days later I headed to sunny Barcelona. I walked into the hostel in the afternoon, and everyone kept asking me if I was going to the game. I had no idea what game they were talking about. It was FC Barcelona against PSG (Paris Saint-Germain), two of the best soccer teams in the entire world. Barcelona lost the last two games against PSG, and now they had a chance for redemption in their home stadium. The streets outside were getting ROWDY. I said fuck it, I'm going to the game. I threw my luggage behind the counter and ran outside to look for a ticket.

I found a ticket outside the stadium and climbed up into the stands. This was the biggest stadium I had ever been in. The place was absolutely roaring. FC Barcelona showed up for a huge victory over PSG. The players joined us in the streets to parade in celebration into the wee hours of the night. By the time I got back to the hostel I still hadn't checked in, so I crashed on the couch in the common area. The next morning I woke up and couldn't find my phone. No phone in a foreign country. At first I was upset, but as the day went on, I realized it was actually really nice. With no distractions, I could take in the city and all it had to offer.

• ‒

Barcelona had a beachy, skater-surfer vibe that reminded me of San Diego. I felt like I was at home. Beautiful churches, beaches, viewpoints, and tapas. The people were laid-back and friendly. Everyone operates on a two-hours-later-than-usual kind of schedule. Businesses open around 10 instead of 8. Siesta, their lunch break, is taken around 2 and lasts until 4. Businesses then reopen and stay open late. The hostel I stayed in was full of travelers from all over the world. Many of them were also solo. I was able to explore the city with Argentinians one day and Australians the next. One night I heard four different languages being spoken at the same time in the common area.

Each night around 10pm, the hostel staff cooked up a "family dinner" that anyone could pitch in to join. At midnight, the locals would take us out to a bar, where we would meet up with other hostels. Around 2am, our gathering would head to a club. Back home clubs are closed by 2am. One night in particular our group had grown to over 100 travelers and hostel staff. The music in Barcelona was a great mix of Spanish music and American hip-hop. I loved it. On the last day, I really wanted to get a tattoo.

The name of the hostel, Sant-Jordi, comes from a Catalan (the region where Barcelona lies) folk tale. Sant-Jordi was a knight who slayed a dragon, which then bled roses. Sant Jordi day is comparable to our Valentine's Day. Locals meet up in the streets and the men offer women roses. The symbol of the hostel was a dragon, so I got a dragon tattooed on my arm, a souvenir to take back home and remind me of the wild adventures and memories from my first successful solo trip in a foreign country.

On my last night in Barcelona I went out to the club, and convinced some girls to go skinny-dipping with me in the Mediterranean Sea. When we got out of the water, it was around 4 am. I had a flight at 8 am that same morning. I ran through the streets of Barcelona to discover the subways had stopped running. I would have to make the trip back to the hostel on foot. I made it back around 6 am, quickly threw everything into my bag, and grabbed a taxi to the airport. I made it there a little past 7. When I checked in, they told me I better run to make the flight. I felt like I had been running for hours. I raced through the airport and made it to the plane just in time. I sat down and immediately fell asleep.

•—• • •— ••• ——— —•

"In my travels I have seen great things. I have met some amazing people. I have experienced some life changing events. Seeing things can possibly be life changing. Meeting people can absolutely be life changing. How can I change people's lives that I come into contact with every day? What kind of message do I want to give to people each day that might resonate within them at such a level that it might influence their thinking or actions in a certain way? That is power."

I've reflected on these thoughts for a while. In my experience, influence is a bit of a paradox. Most people seem to not like being directly told what to do with their life. People value their freedom and autonomy. Instead, sharing my own experiences, or strategies used to upgrade my own life, I may serve as a beacon, through which others may be inspired to find their own path. Encouraging awareness and thoughtfulness might be one of the greatest influences you can bring to another fellow human.

I had a new dream that was starting to brew. I had the dream of becoming a doctor. I wanted it for multiple reasons. No one in my family had ever been a doctor, or gotten a degree that high. Both of my parents grew up in a humble socio-economic class. I wanted to break that class. I knew I had the book smarts to do it, I just needed to find my specific place in the world of practicing medicine. If you don't get into nursing school, it makes sense to apply to med school, right?

Chapter 6:
AZC Rebirth

Ahhhh.... I was back at home and at the beach. But this year I wouldn't be getting paid to have my toes in the sand. I tested positive for cocaine during my medical exam for lifeguarding. I partied the night before and someone reassured me that cocaine would not show up in a piss test. They were wrong. No more lifeguarding.

The next week I got a job bussing tables at Duck Dive, a popular sports bar right next to the sand. The job didn't last long. Two weeks into bussing tables was Cinco de Mayo. I had the brilliant idea to drink on the beach with my friends during the day, before my shift that evening. I remember thinking: "Fuck it, it's Cinco de Mayo." I walked into work absolutely hammered. They told me to go home, and that we would talk next week. I drunkenly obliged and headed home to continue the party. Next week I didn't hear from them. No more Duck Dive.

My roommate, Eli, was a Colombian guy that was into DJing. We both loved to party. Some would say we got along too well. AZC had its first resident DJ. During the day he was running orders for a food delivery service, and said it was easy money. I went from being a lifeguard on the island of Coronado to a food delivery driver in a month. This turn of events made my stomach turn and my pride fall. I felt like my world was crumbling around me. My parents sacrificed so much to build our family a beautiful home and provide me with support and opportunities. I was irresponsibly partying these opportunities away. And to top it off, my "student living" apartment by SDSU was shared by a bunch of crips.

Everything in the house, "on crip" this, on crip that. Burger, on crip. Wipe my ass, on crip. Sometimes there were four guys sleeping in one tiny-ass bedroom. Other times they would break into the spare bedroom to fit four more. Some days they would be locked up, only one or two guys around. They smoked weed and played PlayStation all fucking day. Until they got a lick (robbery) they would move on. One night, a guy came in waving a gun around in the living room. It was around 3am. I was in bed. There was a standoff out in the hallway, no shots fired.

Occasionally I returned home to see my parents, who lived an hour away. It was a breath of fresh air to be in a clean, safe environment. I was afraid to tell my parents how I fucked up. I was afraid of how they would react. Perhaps my memories of the SAT test were being re-lived in my subconscious.

I felt myself sinking deeper into this hole I dug for myself. I knew I needed a change. I needed to place myself on a trajectory towards the bigger goals and dreams that I had for my life. I knew that one day I would share my knowledge, creativity, and wisdom to make the world a better place. I wanted to be the best father (one day), person, and friend that I could be to those around me. I just felt lost in which direction I should step next. I took a deep breath, and told myself to stay strong.

.. '--

I was talking to some friends that had a great deal on mushrooms and molly. Trying these recreationals had been really fun, created a great vibe/mood, and I was fascinated by my experiences on them. I could also sell them for so much profit. It sounded like a no-brainer. I was already comfortable selling weed after my time with Hustle and Jared. So my friends hooked me up with a deal.

I was now delivering food orders and drugs around San Diego. I was hustlin. And it was honestly fun being the plug. Being the guy with the fun candies brought a lot of attention and I was soaking it up.

One of the greatest weekends of my life was at Coachella music festival. I went with Eli and our close friend Nick@Nite, termed for his love of dancing to house music into late hours. The festival really starts on day zero. Everyone sets up camp, then proceeds to get absolutely and irresponsibly hammered. Nick and Eli came to my parents' house in the morning, and we piled into my car for the drive to Indio Valley. Once we got on the road these fools started cracking open Four Lokos. No surprise there. An hour later, Nick was throwing up out the window on the freeway. He told me he made eye contact with another driver while he was unloading. It was 11 in the morning. I was crying from laughter.

At one point I pulled over to take a piss on a tree. While I was peeing, I had the urge to fart. Nothing abnormal there. Until, the fart came out wet. Not only did I feel how wet and warm it was, it also stank more than your usual flatulence. We cruised up to the festival with style. Vomit on the car door, and wet stinky underwear.

Many of my friends from San Diego were camping at the festival. The scene was a non-stop party. The camping area had a silent disco after hours each night. And, we ended up partying with SDSU cheerleaders all weekend. On day one I dropped acid for the first time. I remember the whole crowd folding in on each other. At one point I was climbing uphill on all fours, only to stand up and realize I was in a flat field. Good times. The festival line-up featured DJ Snake, Future, Schoolboy Q, Kendrick Lamar, Nghtmre and Slander. Skrillex came out unannounced at the end of night two and threw down at the DoLab, one of the cooler stages.

. —.. — —

On a typical night around SDSU we would ride out, one designated driver, four in the trunk of my SUV. When one party got "rolled" or shut down by the cops, the whole crowd would dissipate and then recongregate at a new house a few blocks away. It was honestly orchestral some weekends. Sometimes 5+ different houses in a night.

It was weekends like these that compelled me to continue pursuing wild, drug-induced parties and activities. It was great fertile grounds for making friends and hooking up with girls. I continued to party more and more and seek out the lit events on the weekends. I got more AZC merchandise made, hung up the poster again, and started yelling "Alpha Zeta Clutch!!" any time I walked into a bar or a party. AZC was reborn, and it was thriving.

Nick, me, Eli

"Last night I took almost two 8ths of shrooms and then hippie flipped with an Oreo. I traveled to about 6 different planets while I took a shit. I was sauced as hell."

Eli, Dredan and I woke up one morning and decided to make a spontaneous trip to Las Vegas during EDC weekend (Electric Daisy Carnival, the most-attended music festival in the US). The plan? Sneak into EDC. That's it. That was the whole plan. So really, no plan. Just an optimistic idea. Pixie Dust. Dredan was a Jamaican guy full of entertainment. One minute you could find him acting skits without cue and the next having a heart to heart about the meaning of life.

I broke my foot hopping a barbed wire fence while sneaking into EDC. Tried to bribe multiple security guards that all said we had three more checkpoints to get through. Forgot we took mushrooms earlier. Ended up in a wheelchair on the strip with my boys wheeling me around, all 3 of us on a face-load of molly. The whole weekend was a huge L. We didn't get into any clubs since they were crazy expensive, or we were being degenerate chasing girls around. The last morning, Dredan punched the fucking pay box at a parking structure exit. Security rolled out in a golf cart. Dredan smooth-talked, saying it wasn't working, and security told us to have a nice day. Free to go. I had a fever and chills for a week after all the partying that weekend.

• • • • ▬

I met this beautiful, short brunette one night named Emily. Her eyes made me weak, and we got along really well together. She lived in LA, but came down to San Diego occasionally. The next time I saw her, our chemistry had fired up even more. I brought her home with me. Before we got down to it, she asked me three times if I was clean. I didn't have a condom. I told her yes.

That night was maybe the best sex I've ever had in my life. It was the first girl I'd been with that was actually a certified freak. Her dirty talking was off the charts! I was also genuinely into this girl, and hoped to see her again. She was always playing hard to get and said "We'll see."

I got a phone call about two weeks later. It was Emily.

"Armani, tell me why I have chlamydia."

Fuck. "I don't know, it wasn't me."

"Armani, you gave me chlamydia. I haven't been with anyone else. When was the last time you were tested?"

"No way. I mean, I haven't been tested in a while."

"Goodbye Armani. Get yourself tested." Click.

Fuck me. I actually really liked this girl.

I went to get tested and what do you know, I had chlamydia. It turns out that my boy Jesse got it at the same time. There was a girl that had been coming over to our houses, smoking us out, and then boning. It had to have gone between all three of us. I felt awful. I tried calling and texting Emily many times. No reply.

.-.. -.-- ...-. .

I helped throw a fat house party at a friend's pad one night. Nick, Eli, and I were headed back to the apartment for the after-party. Nick was going to drive his car, but I could see that he was way too fucked up. I said I would drive. I had a few drinks, but was in way better shape than he was. We decided to go to the taco shop real quick, an extra ¼ mile drive. Within that ¼ mile I was pulled over for failure to come to a complete stop at a red light before turning right.

I agreed to the sobriety test, which I later found out saved me from additional repercussions. Somehow I recited the entire alphabet backwards and stood on one leg for 27 seconds. My eyes and my line walk were not as impressive. The officer took me to the station.

I blew a 0.12 and ended up in jail for 12 hours. The first time I called, my dad told me to get comfortable there. The second time I called mom and she said they would come bail me out. Eli picked me up downtown when I was finally released. I went back to my car to find the window smashed in and about ⅛ of my wardrobe stolen, including my AZC patched jackets and my gold chains from Mom and Nonni. Fucking shit.

Despite the memories I was making, when the tequila-infused haze wore off the next morning and I started up my car I was reminded of the glamorous, beach lifeguard-life I had left behind. There were days I was driving around just crying. I tried to hold my head up and stay confident that things would turn out ok. But some days it was hard.

I found myself in a suboptimal environment, but I managed to continually tell myself that I was meant for great things. I was praying these small acts of assurance would pay off in the long run. I held onto my dreams, and my belief in my dreams no matter how rough my circumstances became. I was hoping this downward turn of events was only temporary.

Chapter 7:
SHIT!!

The Del Mar horse racetrack hosts San Diego's County fair during the summer. Rides, food, chicks, music, all the greatly overpriced fun stuff we kids love to do. My friends and I invited our neighbor, Jose, to come along for the ride. Jose came over dressed in slacks and a nice button up. I was in ripped jeans, an army jacket, fake chains and a snapback. We logically picked up two huge jugs of Sangria at the drug store and headed out to the show.

We parked in a large lot across the freeway, where you can take a school bus to the entrance. The sangria was almost gone when we approached the bus. We were absolutely belligerent drunk. The passenger population on this bus ride consisted of families, elderlies, and 5 blacked out kids in their early 20s. We were yelling and laughing like uncaged farm animals. A few minutes into the ride, I hear someone yack a load. It was Jose. Seconds later, I was pulling my feet up to the seat as purple sangria slime slid beneath me. The vomit covered a third of the entire bus floor. Jose continues. Dredan was sitting next to him, absolutely losing his shit. He didn't know what to do. I was crying from laughing so hard. Everyone else on the bus was dead silent. A few minutes later, Eli turns to me and says

"Bro I have to piss. NOW."

"Bro, you're gonna have to hold it, we're almost there."

"Fuck that." Eli runs up to the front of the bus, commanding the driver to let him off immediately. The bus guy says "no can do buddy, it's illegal."

"No you don't understand, I have to pee.. now!"

"No can do, buddy."

"Fuck that." Eli shoulders the door open and runs off with high knees for a bush to relieve himself.

When we get off the bus Jose is soaked in sweat, his previously classy slacks are stained with purple liquid and chunks of debris I'd rather not try to guess at naming.

He looks at me and says, "Armani, I feel better now. I'm good to go in." He looked like death.

"Bro, there's no way you're going inside right now. I'll call you an uber home and wait out here with you." I call an uber, help him get in the car, and send a text assuring him I've done much worse and that he's gonna be just fine. We head into the fair to find Eli behind his uncle's booth jumping up and down with a huge smile on his face and two enormous turkey legs in his hands. We throw down some food and then meet up with some girls we'd been crushing on. After a few rides, we decided that our debaucherous behavior would be better suited for a state party.

- - -

My life that summer was a blur of drugs, women, going broke, jail-time, getting fat, pissing off my parents, breaking my foot, letting 3 good jobs slip out of my fingers, and getting a DUI. Needless to say, I was desperate for a grown-up W. It was time for a long-awaited move into my first house. Eli, Drew, and I had been looking for months.

Finding a house on the beach was a whole animal of its own. With some persistence and luck, we landed an amazing little duplex in the middle of Pacific Beach, San Diego. Fucking paradise. I was moving from the crip-infested junk-pile to a beach house. And it felt amazing. My troubles, however, were far from over.

One weekend I needed a form of identification to attend a festival in LA. Since I lost my driver's license during the DUI, I thought it would be easy to pick up my passport at my parents' house on the drive north. Dredan and I left San Diego around 8 or 9 in the morning, tequila already open, raging to dubstep the whole drive up there.

Guy was home, helping Dad mow the lawn and take care of the yard. I walked inside to find Mom and explained to her I was just grabbing a few things. I realized it was the first time I had seen them since my DUI. Mom smelled tequila on my breath. Fuck me. She started crying, asking if I was ok and what I was doing with myself. I told her I had gone out the night before. That was the hardest visit home I ever had. The tequila-infused scent reaffirmed her worries about my downward spiral into a McDonald's career. I grabbed my passport, ran out to Dredan, and quickly reached for the bottle. I was ready to leave this heavy drama behind and party.

I went to the festival with about 60 presses of ecstasy and a half oz of mushrooms. I was gonna be making money this weekend. One of the girls was taking my goodies in and lost 10 presses. Strong start. Early during day one the group was disbanded in the crowd energy. Drew and I went to the trap tent, where there was a huge mosh pit at 3 in the afternoon. We looked at each other. I grabbed him with both hands and threw him towards the pit, then jumped in behind him.

My favorite artists throughout the weekend included Ekali, Skrillex, Snoop Dogg, and Rae Sremmurd. The second day, Leo lost his ticket twice while we were in line. Nick got so fucked up, I didn't think they were going to let him inside the festival. He miraculously stumbled through the entry gates, then proceeded to headbutt Drew while we were dancing, splitting his cheek open. Drew went to the med tent. Eli was throwing up from the drugs not too far from the med tent. So many great memories.

I got a text from my brother the following week. "I don't recognize you as my brother until you get your shit together." My stomach turned. I felt disconnected, and unaccepted for who I was becoming. Perhaps I should say, for the actions and decisions I had been making. Sometimes I wonder if there is a difference. I knew I had to make a change, but I wasn't sure how to go about it. For the first time in my life, I felt loved and accepted by my friends and at the same time judged and unsupported by my family. I knew they wanted the best for me, but I didn't like the way they were showing it.

--- .... .- -. .-

The first weekend in the beach house I naturally threw a party. Eli got sent to the drunk tank, again. Our house was a duplex, featuring a shared backyard with a neighboring duplex. Four households, one fat backyard. We set up the yard with lights, couches, and a fire pit. We quickly became friends with the neighbors, and kept our doors open, making the duplex one big house. We were always excited to see each other and hangout.

"An absolute rollercoaster and I love each piece of it in its own way. At the time, I had been thinking: I'm going to publish this story when I'm a bit older. Life is a mystery of ups and downs. There will be times when your world crashes down around you. There will be times when you're perfectly fine but you just feel like breaking down and crying. There will be times when you feel as if you can take on the entire world. There will be times when you experience such bliss and satisfaction that you never want that moment to end. Accept all of these times how they are, accept winning and losing as it is. Accept happiness and sorrow as they come and go. But keep your head, your purpose, and your respect for yourself and your respect for the people around you high in your heart and soul. Don't listen to anyone. Listen to what everyone has to say. Forge a path that no fucking person in the entire world has ever walked before and let the excitement and energy of that idea overwhelm you as you wake up every day. I am a king."

A typical weekend in the glory of Pacific Beach: As I take a sunset cruise with the windows down, I look out over Mission Bay, the water is smooth as glass. Across from me is a peninsula featuring luxurious houses which cast long blurry lights over the water. You can feel something in the air, or maybe it's the anxiety in my stomach. Either way, I'm about to get home to the little neighborhood called Pacific Beach; the best bar scene in all of San Diego.

Guys high knee to their houses screaming, bottle in hand. Girls sit on the ground and smear shit on their faces for a couple hours. Guys run in the door and start chugging bottles. Putting the stresses of their week behind them as they forget about life for a while in the bliss of their friends and the beauty of the scenery.

For me: I'm running down the street after delivering orders all day. I hear Eli and Drew DJing. Their speakers are shaking half the block. The sunset is a deep orange, and breathtaking. Towering palm trees reach up and decorate the sky. One of my girl friends arrives, jumps on my bed, whips out her new fake tits, and throws some blow on them. Here we go.

Me and Eli

I was always known for throwing great Halloween parties. Halloween 2017 was the one to go down in history. Around 4pm Dredan and I decided to smoke some DMT I had been saving for a special occasion. The shit looked gnarly. A piss-yellow crystal that needed to stay in the freezer. We shared the point, a half-dose each. The effects were subtle at the lower dose. What I didn't expect was the feeling of horse-dog-ape shit afterwards. I assumed the fetal position and passed out in bed until 9.

Eli woke me up, we had a party to throw. I crawled onto my feet, pleasantly relieved at my sobriety. It sounded like a good time for a pull from the handle of Captain Morgan on the table. I rinsed in the shower and threw on a fluffy bathrobe. Improvised Hugh Heffner. The bunnies would slide through later. At 1am over a hundred people were raging at the house. I fucked a girl on top of Drew's car in the garage. Cops showed up and shut it down.

The next morning, I woke up to find my fence destroyed and the toilet in three pieces. Yes, the toilet. In three pieces. Apparently, someone unrolled all the toilet paper and threw it in the bowl. One of the homegirls dug it out with her hands. The following night I got kicked out of two different houses for being absolutely shit faced.

I decided maybe a cleanse from drugs and drinking was a good idea for my life and health. Eli agreed to join me. We lasted until day 5. On day 5, we got wrecked drunk. I broke a girl's nose on the wall while we were hooking up. Eli went hiding under cars down the street and took a 30 minute nap in the alley during the walk back from the taco shop. He walked back into the house covered in dirt and wine, with a goofy grin across his face. Talk about a shit show.

-    -   -

Another night I threw a house party and Carley showed up. Whoopty-fucking-do. I knew I would run into her eventually, we had too many mutual friends. What I didn't anticipate was her trash-talking me to the girls I wanted to hook up with. In my own fucking house. I told her I would kick her out if she kept causing drama.

One night the line for DuckDive (yes, my old job) was so long I was confident I would be waiting at least an hour to get in. All my friends were inside. I went for a smoke and met a guy from the smoking area that said he would pop the window open for me. I slid through the crack in the window, and dropped into a booth where there was a large party sitting down.

"Hey friends. Nice night we're having."

They all froze and looked at me like I was an alien creature. "Good talk, I'm going for a drink!" I meshed in with the bar crowd just before security arrived to investigate their open window.

For my birthday that year we went to an Ekali show in LA. Amazing show. On the drive back, Derrick and I had a long heart to heart about getting my shit together and working towards my goals. My brother (Guy) and I were not talking at this point. He didn't want much to do with me and just had sassy things to say whenever I saw him. Derrick and I talked about how much family meant, and focusing on our dreams and aspirations. I felt like I was ready to show my family that I could be responsible, stay out of trouble, and live up to my potential.

-- · ·- -· ···

Man. It was February and the biggest music festival in San Diego was live for the weekend: CRSSD fest. The venue was in a park downtown, right on the water. It was my first time going and I was beyond excited. I got dropped off to the line where I was looking for my friends. I had a stash of goodies on me and two shooters of alcohol behind my belt. I decided I didn't want to have the shooters right behind my belt. After looking around to ensure the coast was clear, I shoved them in my pants. Dude grabs me randomly. "Undercover, come this way." Fuck. He takes me aside, searches me down, and finds my stash. I was carrying twenty presses of ecstasy. Instead of the much-anticipated festival, I went to jail for 3 days.

Jail was a time of reflection, for sure. I questioned who I want to be and what I want to accomplish. Deep down I knew that this was just one part of my story, and would not define my entire legacy. I was in a cell with two other guys, in a jail block of thirty cells. We could walk around the block for most of the day and were fed three shitty meals. Sometimes it was a bucket of slop and I honestly could not guess what was inside.

I wasn't sure how long I was going to spend in jail. I talked to my cellmates about my charges. Some said I'd be released soon, others said I was looking at two months. It dawned on me that I might be living in four walls of concrete for a while.

Around day 3 I was taken to court, where I was placed in a holding cell. I remember guys snorting drugs in the holding cell literally moments before they were brought before a judge. Crazy. I was informed that my case was being dropped and I would be released later that day. I was ecstatic. When I was finally released, I rushed home, grabbed a bottle of tequila, and hopped over to Mexico to hit the strip club with four birds.

I later found out that my case was being reopened. Apparently, they had to test the drugs before they could press any charges. Suddenly I was in the position to explain to my chemistry professor that I was going to court for selling drugs and it would be a huge help to have a letter of recommendation. He obliged. In court, I ended up with a felony: possession with intent to sell.

When they arrested me I drunkenly agreed to let the cops go through my phone, where they found texts of sales I made that week. Your boy was a felon. Tons of fines, community service, registered narcotics offender, and felony probation. I was not allowed to go to a place where the main thing they sold was alcohol (I still went to the bars every weekend). Another delightful event; I was banned from door dash while I was in jail. Too many recent shenanigans with canceled orders. So, I was also unemployed. I quickly got a job at Jersey Mike's where some friends worked.

- - -

That summer Eli and I were in the position to get a new house. We couldn't renew the last one since we had too many noise complaints from our late-night parties. We found a dope spot and were filling out applications. I remember looking at my bank account and I had negative five dollars. I texted Eli and laughed. Then it sank in. I didn't even have money to turn in an application for a house. The weight of my recent missteps threw me down towards the ground. I felt ashamed for the mess I found myself in. I was a big believer in a strong mindset and attitude, but this was not an easy time to get through.

One day in particular will always be etched into the fragments of my memory. I woke up hungover and drove to one of my favorite beaches in La Jolla. I didn't want to be hungover, I felt like dog shit. I dropped into the sand in child's pose.

My first job had been on a beautiful beach, and the memories of those glorious work days flooded my mind. I thought about the opportunities I threw away. The recent jail time echoed around each memory. Reflecting on the last few years of my life was like setting a blade on fire and slowly plunging it into my soul. I started shaking. Sobbing. I didn't even care about the drool that was spurting from the corners of my mouth. I begged for the forgiveness of the sand, and the tenacity of the ocean. I prayed for help.

I put my head down and started grinding like I never had before. I received a promotion and a raise within six days of working at Jersey Mike's. I was taking organic chemistry in the fall and was determined to crush it. I woke up a few hours before work each day and watched Khan Academy videos to prepare for the class. This was one of the best decisions I ever made. I started meditating before class and visualizing myself being attentive, participative, and confident. The effects of this simple strategy were much more profound than I anticipated.

..-. .- -- .. .-.. -.--

One thing that I noticed when I stopped selling drugs: I felt kind of lonely. Perhaps I used the identity of selling drugs as a medium to connect with people. My phone was quiet during class, as I had significantly less people hitting me up during the day. I also had been running my own business which was rewarding in its own way. I felt like I lost both a sense of identity and a community. My phone seemed unnaturally quiet. In class I wasn't yet comfortable being the social butterfly I embodied at the bars.

Chapter 8:
Every Action has a Reaction

"Success is walking from failure to failure with no loss of enthusiasm." -Winston Churchill

On my drives to work I started listening to Audible. This started a snowballing effect on my acquisition and application of knowledge. I stumbled upon a book titled "Own the Day, Own your Life" by Aubrey Marcus. Aubrey was a fan of a strong morning routine, and a healthy balance of work, movement, and fun throughout the day. Mimi Guarneri's "The Science of Natural Healing" also had a great influence on me. Dr. Guarneri is a cardiologist who has an integrative clinic in La Jolla. I was surprised to discover her practice was only a ten minute drive from my house. I reached out to her office, asking how I could get involved in this realm of natural, holistic healing. I heard back from the office a week later with a suggestion to join the Academy of Integrated Health and Medicine (AIHM).

AIHM is a large social network of healers from students to nurses and docs. Dr. Guarneri happened to be a past president. My first event with them was a networking event at her clinic. I was fortunate to meet many students who were studying at Bastyr University in San Diego. This was the first time I'd ever heard of Bastyr. I would later find out that this prestigious university was the leader in naturopathic medicine in the country. You can say they had my attention.

The night before this networking event, I had been out drinking. Heavily. While I was at the event, I suddenly felt light headed. Moments later I woke up lying down on the floor. I passed out. Again. Some ladies helped me into a more private room nearby to sit down and have something to drink. Before I knew it, Mimi Guarneri herself was sitting next to me, feeling my pulse and sharing her interpretation. I felt like a fanboy, the first thing I said was how much I loved her book HAHA. The rest of the event went fine, and although I managed to embarrass myself, I returned home eager to look into Bastyr.

Passing out had been a problem for me since 5th grade when I passed out on my desk while taking a test. If I remember correctly, no one had even noticed. It usually happens every few years, in a variety of situations: a boy scouts interview, at home, while giving a speech in freshman year of high school. That one was a charmer; I fell down, lost consciousness, had a dream, and gloriously peed my pants.

About two weeks after the networking event, I was studying organic chemistry with a friend at a Starbucks. This time I fell and hit my head. I was taken to the ER. My parents met me there, and what do you know my mom looked through my paperwork to read that I tested positive for cocaine. Fuckkkk. My parents, once again, saw me messing around with drugs. As if two trips to jail wasn't enough already. It had been roughly one year since I was arrested for ecstasy.

The doctor ordered me to do follow up visits with a heart and brain specialist. I even wore a heart monitor for two weeks. Nothing notable was found. I took a month off of drinking, which was really great for me. My creativity in the classroom shot through the roof. At the time I was reading Joe Dispenza, who had a profound impact on me and my thinking. His book, "You are the Placebo" goes in-depth about just how powerful our thoughts are, and the stories we tell ourselves. I started to stretch and meditate in the mornings. I created daily goals and reflected on them before I went to bed. Perhaps my health problems, and my interest in health, started pushing me onto a path towards self-improvement and away from the desires of the party scene.

..

When I was a kid, my father would tell me "Every action has a reaction". Those words still echo in my head today. Initially, I thought I understood what he was saying. A turn too hard on a skateboard with improper speed means you're gonna eat shit. As I got older, I noticed this same concept applied to deeper decisions such as; who you surround yourself with, or the activities you choose to take part in. The action of attending conferences placed me in an environment where dreams, ambitions, intellectual conversation, and creative ideas flowed like water. Getting up early in the morning and connecting to my mind, body, and spirit was an action that produced the reaction of having a more intentional day. I was able to show up with more energy, vitality, and purpose.

I eventually applied and was accepted to Bastyr in Seattle, on a scholarship. At first I was hesitant about going to an expensive, private school. I called up my boy Kunal, who was going to the University of San Diego (USD), also an expensive private school. This champion of a man had been diagnosed with cancer a few years ago. He moved back home to get healthy, and after he recovered got a FULL RIDE to study neurobiology!

We sat down for coffee at USD and he asked me to write out a pros-and-cons list of my school options. The other schools I applied to were public schools (less expensive) in California. The one I was most serious about, and had been accepted to was Long Beach. When I wrote out the list, it was clear to me that Bastyr was the most resonant with my soul, the most aligned with my career goals, and the school that would most support the healthy personal growth I was looking for.

After sitting down with Kunal for a while, I really had to take a leak. Like, really really had to take a leak. I told him I had to go bad. The nearest bathroom was maybe a half a mile away across campus. We started walking together at a reasonable pace. I gradually picked up the pace to a jog.

"Bro, you're gonna make it fine. Slow down."

"Bro, I don't think you understand. I might not make it to the bathroom."

I started running. As I turned the corner into the building, I had 50% confidence that I would make it. I had to ask two people where the bathroom was, holding my knees together like a 5 year old. I find the bathroom, rush inside like a madman, and FUCK. I didn't make it. Piss bursts from my cucumber, wetting my underwear. I whip it out a few steps before the urinal, trying to clamp the stream in, but it sprays out onto the floor.

As the moment of relief comes, I gasp for air as if I was held under by a 15 foot wave. The obscenely ridiculous nature of my predicament was undoubtedly embarrassing, but at the moment all I could do was laugh at my situation. I just sat down and had a sophisticated discussion about private school scholarships, but the nature of the human animal had me running around the schoolyard and pissing my pants.

.− −. .. ..

I was talking to a homie about the Electric Daisy Carnival (EDC) one night. He told me his dad worked for Corona and he was confident he could get us tickets. A week later, I had a free VIP ticket secured for the most-attended musical festival in the world. And, I was going back to Vegas. Hehe.

The festival was fun as hell. I got excited and took way too much molly. I rolled all three nights on doses good enough for 2-3 people each night. My semester finals took place right after the festival. I completely missed making it back to take my organic chemistry final Monday night. Thankfully, my professor met me on campus two days later so I could take it. I was also having weird eye and ear spasms that week. When I tried to sleep, my ears would get a blasting ringing noise and bright lights flashed before my eyes. I for sure did way too many drugs. I felt depressed. At the time, I thought I had truly fucked myself for transfer to Bastyr.

.− −−. .− .. −.

My last summer in San Diego was epic. Beach, sunshine, girls, and the summer that hard seltzers made an epic delivery. I was cranking out community service in the mornings twice a week, picking up trash on the freeway, then heading into Jersey Mike's for a shift. Those were 15 hour days. I was thankful for the experiences I had in San Diego during the last 5 years. I felt I had truly grown. In a full circle kind of way. Despite how stressful my predicaments became, I made an effort to stay grateful for the simple things like having clean drinking water every day. I am honored to call myself Armani Antonellis, second generation Italian-American, owner of many nicknames, friend to all, asker of questions, doing the improbable, first of his name.

It was about one week from the day I planned to move up to Washington. I was legally not allowed to leave the county of San Diego without authorization from probation. I had completed extra community service, paid off all my fines early (thanks to Dad), and now had the final court hearing to amend my probation terms, ending it two years early. This would allow me to move up to Seattle and pursue my dreams of an education in integrative health care.

The morning of my court date I woke up with no letters of recommendation, despite reaching out to multiple mentors. I got a hold of Josh, my supervisor at work and he (bless his soul) hustled to put together an un-detailed letter in an inaccessible format. I also waited for his revision but when the whole thing was a sloppy mess, and I was running low on time, I said fuck it and ran out the door.

I sat in court for two hours listening to fellow humans in custody have their jail times extended. I was ready to speak to the judge personally in case I missed my chance for a public defender, but eventually realized I wouldn't have to. When my case was called, the judge was at first skeptical since it was a drug related charge. Hell, before that, even the public defender was skeptical about the whole reduction and about how early I was requesting this action to be done. However, the District Attorney had no objection.

The probation officer representative even commended me: "This is exactly the thing we love to see from kids on probation. Pursuing higher education and getting their feet back on track. These are the outcomes we hope for as probation officers."

The judge, hearing of my scholarly efforts, and the angelic recommendation, agreed to drop the charge to a misdemeanor and end probation. I was a FREE MAN!! So pumped!! I received a ton of love and support from friends and family when they heard. It was a great feeling thinking I would not have to step into court again. This was my sixth court appearance in the last two years. A weight had been lifted off of my shoulders. My head was held high, and my eyes shone bright, excited to launch into the next chapter of my life. My goal was to get A's across the board while at Bastyr the next two years.

Chapter 9:
Pacific Northwest

Bastyr University

Holy shit. What an absolute blessing Bastyr University was for me. Many of my fellow classmates had mixed experiences here, but for me it was exactly what I needed at this stage of my life. Within my second quarter, I was leading meditations on campus, involved in a student research project with prostate cancer and an herbal formula, in an official club named "Bastyr Masterminds". I developed stronger student-teacher relationships than ever before, led group study sessions, joined a Toastmasters club off-campus to develop my public speaking skills, I started writing this book, did a handstand, accomplished more networking than ever before in my life, and nailed all A's both quarters.

When I moved to Bastyr I was 24 years old, and I finally had my own room out of my parents' house. While I was in San Diego, I had started to experiment with my morning routine, but it was often hindersome since I didn't have a bedroom to myself to stretch and meditate. A few weeks into Bastyr I found a great routine that I continue to utilize to this day and has possibly been the most effective daily tool I have ever found.

Wake up 6:30
Roll out of bed, take a piss, drink some water
Stretch, yoga. Focus more breaths on areas that are tight
Meditate 15 min
Walk through the forest listening to an audiobook
Wim Hof shower

About a month into school I took a "weekend intensive", a one weekend class, called wild crafting. Suzanne (the instructor) took the class into protected forestland, where she paid a couple G's just for a key into the access road. She showed us her integrative wilderness first aid kit, full of homeopathic remedies, tinctures, oils, and more. The second day we made elixirs, oxalems, and honeys. We harvested herbs such as the licorice fern, which grows out of the moss of a big leaf maple tree. Suzanne would pull one out, moss and soil still in the root, and take a bite to indulge in the sweetness.

We all sat in a circle and chopped up onions, ponderosa pine, Doug fir, elderberries, ginger, and citrus as we crafted our own health infusions. At the end of the day she introduced us to mugwort, which is in the same family as moxa (the herb used to treat my knee) and has a variety of uses including promoting lucid dreaming. I dried a bunch at home and tried smoking some with my roommate, but I didn't get the kind of lucid dreams I had when I was a kid.

−·−− −−− ···− ʼ·−· ·

During spring break of 2020 I went to the beach with a bunch of friends and took a kayak out on the Puget Sound. In the distance, I could hear a harmonica. I never felt more immersed in the native lifestyle of the Pacific Northwest than kayaking over the cool water, looking up at the towering pines, a gorgeous colorful sunset over the Olympic mountains, and hearing a harmonica echo over the waves. Around the fire friends shared stories and had heart to hearts.

I had my own heart to heart with one of my neighbors on campus. Reuben went to a fine arts high school in New York, and was well in-touch with his creative and feminine energies. Initially I held some judgment against him, maybe because I didn't understand him. Or because he had a much different background than my SoCal competitive water polo roots. Earlier that week I had been guided in a meditation, and the leader instructed us to send loving energy to someone. I chose Reuben, since I wanted to share love and camaraderie with him, but wasn't sure how. Meditation felt like a good place to start.

While we were together around the fire on the beach, Reuben came up to me and confessed that he held judgment against me, but now that we had gotten to know each other more he had a lot of love for me. I felt my spirit stir, my prior judgments falling aside to make place for compassion. We talked for a while, and decided to embark on a day of darkness together.

Aubrey Marcus had inspired me to dive into the darkness. He spent a whole week without light. I chose to start with one day. A full 24 hours with no light exposure, no use of the human's most vital sense. It was a spiritual journey, a challenge, a means for getting comfortable with being uncomfortable. The day was very peaceful, meditative, slow-moving in a way, as my nervous system was stripped of its regular stimulation. I started locating objects by sound more acutely. Reuben and I had some friends on campus help with food and not running into walls.

A few years ago for spring break I was taking body shots off stripper's melons in Mexico. Now my break was filled with reiki sessions, spinal adjustments, writing, reading, and, kind of oddly, a virtual rave-a-thon. We were just getting into the COVID quarantinas. Big events were canceled, and classes transitioned to online.

.‒   .‒‒ .. ‒‒.. .‒ .‒. ‒..

Wow. The universe really sang to me up in Seattle. I'll give you a few examples:

1.   I had been striving for a process-driven mentality. I read a chapter in a textbook diving into the power of being process driven. It talked about the pomodoro effect, essentially working for 20 minutes and then taking a 5 minute break to maximize your attentive focus and productivity. Guy recently gifted me an audio book detailing the dynamics of deep work. It is wild that when you pursue things for your soul, the universe will answer back to you. Part of the beauty and the magic was the realization that out of all things Guy could have sent me, it happened to be on the same week and discussing the same idea.

2.   I mentioned earlier that I was hesitant about going to an expensive private school. By this time, I had no doubt in my mind that I had made an excellent decision. I had immersed myself in a new environment, one that I had been craving. The flow of ideas and people that were similar to my own exponentiated my personal development. By choosing a more optimal environment, decision making was easier, I was no longer struggling with the chaotic mess of my former party lifestyle. Dr. Martzen explained to us how we can't exist separate, or outside, of our environment. I was seeing how true these words really are.

3. I was testing the effects of garlic and turmeric on breast cancer cells in a class, and was hungry to dive into some formal research. One night for dinner a student from the village was over and we started talking about research. I said that I was interested in doing some lab work while I was at school. He gave me the ins on what kind of support and challenges I could expect from each research mentor. My RA was in the kitchen to help with descriptive scientific terminology. I picked out Dr. Meng since she liked to get the ball rolling quickly and had a lot of publications under her belt. I was told she had high expectations and a bit of a language barrier. I said bet, after saying yes to those hellish swim sets this should be a walk in the park. It was.

.— .—. —— .— —. ..

"Wow, my frequency is buzzing right now. I just attended my first Fireside gathering- by yours truly Sahar. She brought a guest speaker named Bruce. He is a seasoned hunter, and shared his ideas and approach to hunting and the intimate spiritual connection that is cultured through his craft. He shared a story of hiking through the snowy Rocky's all day (all week, really) to finally catch a glimpse of some elk and to hunt it and skin it and hang the meat in a tree as there was no daylight left and he was 3 miles from camp. Over the next 4 days he was able to tow the meat back to his truck and then home. When he brings the elk out onto the table it is such a different connection with the food. The energy in the room tonight was warm, welcoming, curious, and exciting. I met Joey, a local 4th/5th grade teacher in the bathroom and sat next to him for the talk. He teaches his students in a way that encourages awareness of the world around us, and a deeper understanding of our ancestors and their wisdom. How beautiful. I also just finished my latest casual read last night, and the next book on my shelf is The Omnivore's Dilemma. The world continues to amaze me in how things line up in this way. Bruce was

so generous as to offer everyone there - about 40 - to come with him on his Shellfish Gathering and Cooking weekend next month. He told us not to worry about the price. This community at Bastyr is truly magical, and I'm so grateful to have gotten my letter to attend this wizarding school; a fainting spell at Guarneri Integrative Health."

My favorite class I took at Bastyr was "Spirituality and Health". We spent the entire quarter discussing the definition of spirituality. It was run Socratic-seminar style. All of the fifteen students had plenty of time to take the floor, share their thoughts, expand on their experiences, and arrive at conclusions. In that class I learned about the 7 chakras from a Sanskrit perspective. I was introduced to a beautiful meditation that focused on your left foot receiving energy from mother Earth's roots, channeling your chakras up one side, down the other, and through your right foot, where the energy is returned back to Mother Earth. I had a full lecture on acid, ketamine, mdma, dmt, ayahuasca, and mushrooms. I've never had a class where the students actually stay seated after the allotted class time. We went 10 minutes over... many times. And most people had another class that started in 10 minutes.

In the same class I gave an hour and a half long presentation on Native American spirituality and its role in healing. I have always felt drawn to Native American culture. They seem so connected to the Earth and its beauty. I spoke about how a rich man in their culture was seen as someone who had many friends, instead of someone who had many possessions. Their healers would gather a patient's family to participate in healing rituals. Often they would call upon the power of a spirit animal which was believed to have healing abilities. As an example, the spirit of a falcon might be called upon to cast out the power of an infectious snake spirit which was believed to be causing stomach distress in the patient. It is the belief that this healing works that is the most important step.

I felt alive and engaged while learning at Bastyr. I also felt like I was living out my childhood dream of attending

Hogwarts. Bastyr is about as close as you can get in real life. The school is in the middle of a forest, on top of Lake Washington. I walked by a huge willow tree every day on my way to class. And, there were all kinds of unconventional healing practices that one might regard as magical.

Chapter 10:
The Perimeter

"Whether you think you can, or you think you can't, you're right." -
Henry Ford

I had been contemplating what kind of impact I want to have on society through my work. I thought; if I chose an MD/PA/hospital kind of route, I would be in an environment to make a small impact on improving our (mostly) flawed health care system. This may have a longer term effect on many, many lives. Or, I could choose a small-scale, holistic route where I would be in an environment to have a great impact on a smaller number of lives. This impact would be more personal, and more profound on a case-by-case basis.

As I continued to dream and contemplate the future, I shared my ideas with my little bro. My relationship with Guy grew stronger than ever in the last year. We were talking on the phone one day and he expressed that he didn't want to exchange material gifts with each other at Christmas that year. Instead, he wanted to write a detailed goals list, a bucket list, full of life-long dreams and ambitions. I was in. Sounded great.

Goals

He is versed in 3 varieties of ancient medicine - (Ayurveda, Hippocrates, TCM, Egyptian)
He can speak a native language in 3 continents of the world
He has clogged a toilet in 10 countries
He once helped a family in need in a developing country
He transcended a sea with the wind
Both his publications have helped propel the field of medicine
With one speech, he reaches 1,000 ears
His guitar sings to him
Life wrote his autobiography
He once refused to eat food for 10 days
He loves to dance, on his hands
He climbed 3 mountains
He performs a split... without using a banana
He is the life of parties he's never attended
The soil thanks his garden for its presence (more than 10 plants)
He falls upwards
Salmon rejoice when they find his spear
He once parallel parked a train
He once took an astronaut flying
Meditation asked him for awareness on its retreat
His piss pisses on Niagara Falls
He once surfed a wave 4 times taller than he is
His greatest achievement is changing one person's life in a small way

I don't always drink wine, but when I do, I prefer my own.
He is...

Complete 5 by age 30
5 more by 35
5 more by 40

Some of these goals were just jokes, like "His piss pisses on Niagara Falls". Some of them were exaggerated, like "He has clogged a toilet in 10 countries". I wanted to keep the list in the theme of the most interesting man in the world, inspired by the Dos Equis commercials. I always thought they were the greatest commercials ever made. In keeping with the absurdity of his supposed feats, my list read with a louder roar, and a magical touch.

... .- -.--

I shared this list of goals at Bastyr Masterminds, and encouraged others to do the same. My brother and I had been staying in touch with our progression. He expressed interest in creating a group of friends where we could have similar conversations. A group that met with sacred intention, a group that got together not just to hit the bars, get clobbered, and chase tail. I liked how he was thinking. It was also incredibly refreshing to hear from him. I remembered just a few years ago I was begging him to let more people into his life. He was now bringing people in, and inviting me along for the ride.

We talked to some of our high school teammates about the group. We ended up meeting with them on video calls. COVID was coming in at full force at this time, and many things were being done via online video calls. We decided to call ourselves - The Perimeter.

Throughout history men have drawn a perimeter around the land they inhabited. Family and belongings were kept inside. As well as morals, values, and culture. Predators and threats were kept outside. Threats to physical as well as spiritual safety. In modern society and human culture, especially in America, we face fewer physical threats but perhaps more threats to our morals and values. The convenience culture of being able to get anything you need with a tap on your phone has led many to become complacent. The flood of stimuli and dopamine through the incredible phone apps take hold of our energy and cause many to become "zombied".

In The Perimeter we started talking about what morals and values are most important to us. What things do we want to protect and hold sacred within our group? After many discussions we decided on the core values of "Mastery, Brotherhood, Legacy". Mastery of ourselves, brotherhood with each other, and a legacy of impact to the world around us. We eventually started group workouts, camping trips, discussions, book readings, and goal-setting meetings. We paired up as accountability partners, which was especially impactful for me.

While I was in school, I would text my accountability partner:

"Yo if I don't finish my essay by Thursday, I owe you 300 pushups on Friday."

"Bet. You got it bro."

I continue to invite others onto my team to help me reach my goals. It gets them at least a little emotionally invested and it keeps you more consistent. I intentionally designed the punishments to indirectly push me towards other goals, or do something challenging to get me out of my comfort zone.

These bucket-list goals overall went very well. I even knocked the first bucket-list level goal out of the way during quarantine, "He refused to eat food for 10 days".

This path was most certainly not taken smoothly. I was, and still am today, confronting the same demons that plagued me in the past. I fell victim to a cycle of getting really drunk, taking molly, staying up and partying all night, and then waking up the next day absolutely defeated. No energy, no motivation. I would order a pizza and play video games for the day, skipping my workout and studying. I would enter the week on Monday drained instead of refreshed.

I started to question whether it was possible for me to have a casual social night that included drinking? Am I able to just have two or three drinks and go to bed early? Am I destined to continue drinking every time to the point of a hangover? At the time, I honestly wasn't sure.

Abnormal use, or abuse, is such a present thing in our lives. A few years ago, a good friend shared his thoughts; everyone has an addiction to something. The trick is, to make your addictions productive. For example, gym time or producing music. Unhealthy addictions might be pussy or drugs.

Personally, I think that addiction to anything can be harmful. Addiction to work can be unquestionably harmful to your overall being. Studying too long can become an abuse, or unhealthy practice because of the law of diminishing returns and for a similar reason as work: you need overall well-being.

Diving into things you're passionate about, if they are healthy, can be good in certain doses. However, unhealthy use of video games, unhealthy use of food, misuse of Netflix, these things can all be deteriorating. Especially during your fourth hour of video games, you are becoming brain-fried, and don't have nearly as much organic enthusiasm as when you started.

My tendency to overindulge in or misuse entertainment, food, or substances was probably the number one contender in things holding me back from my dreams. During periods of sobriety I was impressively productive, sharp, focused, and strong. Meditation was certainly an invaluable tool to me, it helped me be more aware of my urges. I used to have 15-20 drinks a night, hell Eli and I would split a HANDLE some nights...

Quarantine made things even worse. I wasn't able to see my friends. I was holed up inside my bedroom, where it was easy for me to get pizza and beer and watch movies. Then stay up all night with energy drinks playing video games.

—·—— · ··· — ———

One day I was just scrolling through Instagram and saw a post by Anthony. I played water polo with this guy in community college. He had a huge ego and always talked and acted like he was above everyone else on the team, despite not having the skills in the pool to back it up. The post was a poor quality photo of him in a superhero stance, claiming that some may see him as crazy but alcohol has led him and his friends to believe that he is an embodiment of Aquaman. My initial reaction was one of disgust, and pity. I remembered when Anthony claimed he was the only player on the team during halftime. I always struggled to connect with him.

I now had this realization that maybe these ego imbalances or disconnections are a result of a past trauma in his life that is echoing into his present/future being. Wow, and also that he is an existential force of myself in a different life. That we are all one, and he has experienced things in his past that have shaped his ideas and beliefs.

For the first time I no longer saw him as this conceited oaf living a complete lie, celebrating minute victories in low-competition polo. I now saw him as someone who maybe was never nurtured a certain way to develop his ego. I didn't see this as something that is wrong, but that it just is. I think having an adverse childhood event is inarguably not ideal, but it is a reality. I theorized that if we continue to seek meaning out of events we find ourselves in, undesired events also hold their place in the greater order of the universe.

Neither of us is better than the other, we just have different paradigms through which we walk or swim, or play polo. For the first time in my life I felt like I connected with Anthony. He met a bout of success in his life, and for the first time I empathized with celebratory victory. I no longer resented the fibers of his being, as I realized they were also the fibers of my own being.

This ego disconnection that us humans can place on people can be utterly disastrous. At the end of the day, we all long to feel loved and accepted. Love is creative and supportive. Hate is destructive and repressive.

─·─· ···· ·─ ·─·· ·─·· · ─· ──· · ···

As I came to these realizations, I sought out meditation gurus to learn from. Chandresh Bhardwaj, a Buddhist guru, was especially impactful. I listened to many podcasts before taking his prompt to reach out to him on Instagram for advice. I sent him a dm and explained who I was and what I was looking for in my meditation practice. We ended up crafting a mantra that I could repeat to myself during my meditations. When your mind gets into a meditative state, you can tap into your unconscious mind more easily. By feeding your subconscious mind with a mantra, you can plant seeds and intentions that will continue to work and grow for you during your regular, conscious-mind occupied day. We settled on:

"My intention is to cultivate a deeper understanding and knowledge of medicine every day in every way. I am open to opportunities from both the known and unknown ways."

I repeated this mantra during my morning meditations for a few months, and my grades thanked me for it. When I got home and knew I had studying to do, the action of studying became easier. I knew deep down that studying would be fruitful for me, and it took less effort to become engaged in my studies.

Chapter 11:
Get Some

"Our deepest fear is not that we are inadequate. Our deepest fear is that we are powerful beyond measure. It is our light, not our darkness that most frightens us. We ask ourselves, 'Who am I to be brilliant, gorgeous, talented, fabulous?' Actually, who are you not to be? You are a child of God. Your playing small does not serve the world. There is nothing enlightened about shrinking so that other people won't feel insecure around you. We are all meant to shine, as children do. We were born to make manifest the glory of God that is within us. It's not just in some of us, it's in everyone. And as we let our own light shine, we unconsciously give other people permission to do the same. As we are liberated from our own fear, our presence automatically liberates others." -Marianne Williamson.

Since school was online due to COVID, I moved back to Murrieta, CA. I had mixed feelings about living with my parents again, but it turned out to be one of the best years of my life. I was able to rekindle meaningful friendships with childhood friends, and since mom and dad had an early bedtime, I was getting good sleep and working out like a monster. I had spare time on my hands so I learned the ins and outs of cryptocurrency, got involved in Toastmasters; a huge public speaking club, read books, and worked on projects around the house for Dad to earn some spending cash.

I heard about a weekend conference put on by NMSA (Naturopathic Medical Student Association). I signed up right away. One of the key speakers was Tyna Moore. She had a dual degree in Naturopathic and Chiropractic medicine. Woahhh!! Besides being a doctor, she ran a podcast about natural healing. I was listening to her podcast all week. Some of the talks during the conference were good, but the best part was the opportunity to 'walk with a doc'.

Who would have thought I would get 40 minutes of one-on-one time with THE Tyna Moore. I was able to pick her mind for wisdom and insight. My favorite question in an interview setting is "What books have you been reading lately?" You get to know the interviewee a bit more and you might walk away with a recommendation for another life-changing book. Tyna had been reading a book investigating leadership principles found in the characters from Game of Thrones. I liked her style.

Her opinion about my entry into grad school was surprisingly refreshing. She was explaining how a medical degree is not anywhere near the value that it costs. She is still paying off her loans, 12 years out of school, and from what I could tell she was an incredibly successful doc. Over 3k a month in loans... It had me thinking about the interests I have in medicine, and how I want to help people.

I also got to meet with an OG doc, Maurice Werness, who is aggressively straight up with his accountability. He shares his personal number with patients so they can text him each day with updates on their healing journey. He even gave me his number and said to stay in touch. He told a teary-eyed story about how he found meditation and was able to reach further into his potential and happiness. He said the greatest thing he got from Bastyr was the friendships that he made there. Communication, meditation, companionship: tenets of holistic healing.

—·· ·—· · ·— ——

When I was a lifeguard, we practiced something called preventative lifeguarding. Meaning, we had to be three steps ahead of the game. We communicated early, and helped people stay in safe waters instead of having to Usain Bolt into the water for a close-call rescue. The problem: which one attracts more attention? Which one gives you a fat rush of adrenaline? Which one brings you cheers, hugs, and high fives as you run back to your tower? I made a rescue today!! It was a great day!

Vs

Rock contacts. The least glamorous lifeguard activity. Every 30 minutes I would slowly jog out to the water to monotonously tell another family they couldn't swim there. I assured them it says so on one of the 10 signs right in front of their beach spot, and the 20 orange cones I set up that morning to try to make it even more obvious. Neither of which they saw, of course. Boring. Repetitive. No high fives. Whiny patrons instead of cheering ones. Comparable to traffic ticket glory as a cop.

The truth is, 'the rocks' are potentially one of the most dangerous places on the beach. A few jagged rocks hidden underwater meant one false dive and a split open head. Despite working the rocks countless days, the worst I saw was a few cut toes. From the preventative rock contacts, countless beach-goers were also saved from being stung by stingrays (grown men would be screaming in pain). It was not easy work, but it was prevention at its core, and many people stayed safe because of it.

I propose preventative medicine might be viewed through a very similar lens. Non-invasive changes to your health such as: diet. Something a lot of people don't want to hear about. It's hard to actually make a diet change. Sometimes confusing. Sometimes bitter.

We have been falsely led to believe in the "big rescues" of medicine. The get out of jail free cards. But is there really a get out of jail free card in life? Everything happens for a reason. Your heart is failing because of the things you've been feeding it and the exercise you have partaken or failed to take in during the last 40 years. Insurance companies will cover many prescriptions and primary care visits. Since naturopathic medicine is not widely understood, a visit to such a doc will not be covered by your plan.

This is comparable to not having those preventative jogs from the tower, and relying solely on having the rescues in the dangerous waters. We have taken down the rock signs and cones, and let people split their heads open, so we can then charge them money for a 'glamorous' head surgery. This whole situation is very complex and has developed over many years of money going into the wrong places, to the point where the nutrition industry, artificial corn syrup, and drugs now control the general populace. We don't necessarily have our health in our own hands.

These realizations lead me to strongly believe in the power of holistic medicine and healing. Western medicine has its strengths, but it also has its weaknesses.

Nobody wants to listen to rock contacts. Nobody wants to listen to diet recommendations. They both have subtle effects that don't grab attention, high fives, or adrenaline. They have more subtle, long-lasting effects. Perhaps Dr. Werness has the business on lock with his texting accountability.

In a convenience culture where we are flooded with superficial stimuli, how on Earth can we be expected to look deeper, stay disciplined, and dare to engage with these preventative methods? Health care needs change. It has gotten to the point where these naturopathic methods have been labeled as 'quackery' and their subtle methods have been labeled as fake medicine, a scam. What is the real scam here?

.— —. —.. —... . .—.. .. . ...— .

After reading "The Chiropractic Way", another influential book in my life, I was deeply intrigued by chiropractic medicine. I wanted to see it practiced first hand, so I reached out to local chiropractors to come in for some shadowing.

One chiropractor, Dr. Jim, left an impression on me. He ran a small, family-owned business. He worked 25 hours a week and went home for lunch and/or nap every day. He also had plenty of time to raise a family and train for Ironman triathlons. What a lifestyle. It was the friendliest doctor's office I've ever been to. Dr. Jim knew everyone by first name and gave them a hug as they walked in. Around the boys he swore like a sailor and the kids were swung around the adjusting table twice before they left the office. I was excited to see more.

Despite Tyna Moore's warnings concerning graduate school, becoming a doctor meant a lot to me. I would be the first in my family with the title. I thought back to my visit to Italy, and the humble beginnings my grandparents endured before they immigrated to America. I wanted to do it for myself, and also for my deceased Italian ancestors.

.. —.

One morning in The Perimeter, a meme of Jocko Willink, a former Navy SEAL, was shared. It had an exaggerated description of his morning routine that went something like this:

-sleep on hardwood floor with no pillow
-alarm goes off at 1am
-immediately kip up and scream LETS GET IT
-shower with liquid nitrogen
-shave with a large hunting knife
-for breakfast, 6 egg shells and 4 banana peels
-waterboard myself to build pain tolerance
-easy workout today, do 5000 pushups and 2000 pull ups
-ready for the day at 2am

I shared it with some friends and some of them were like... bro wtf. I was like... bro FUCK YES!! It's not about the numbers that are displayed. It's all about the energy and mindset that is associated with getting up ahead of the pack with absolute determination to crush the day in the best way possible. Jocko had been posting his watch saying 4:30 am for a while with just a few words in all caps... GET SOME. I also woke up at 4:30 that morning and immediately thought of Jocko. Needless to say, I was up and ready to crush it.

‒·‒‒ ‒‒‒ ··‒ ·‒·

"I was invited to go to Mexico for a friend's birthday this weekend. Apparently they have a suite reserved at Hong Kong (a strip club in Tijuana, Mexico) and they're heading down to Rosarito. A year or two ago, I would have been sprinting out the door to go join them. Recently, I've really been thinking about the people I have

around me, the influence that environment instills, and how that aligns with my dreams and desires. Yes, I want to have fun and be social. No, I don't want to do drugs every weekend. STALLION OUT."

That weekend, I instead went down to La Jolla cove in San Diego and swam the gatorman with Chris, Talon, Jake and Guy (all of us played water polo in high school together). The gatorman is a 3 mile ocean swim. In high school we swam it once a year with our coach. Back then it was a brutal workout. Now we were doing it for fun. A few days later I expressed gratitude for:

Oceanside's diversity
The influence of my parents
Guy's commitment to bettering himself
Jake's willingness to attack challenges that push him to failure
Birds chirping in the morning

I am rejoicing in not going down to San Diego to party with drugs anymore.

I remember this last line being hard for me to write. There was a part of me that still identified with being a party animal. I realized the change had to start with a thought pattern, with an idea, and then it became a first step. Writing it down made it become even more real. I believe it will become a little easier to write each time, until I can rewire my subconscious habits that have been driving some of my actions. It's interesting that many of my big life changes took shape once I wrote them down. Going to Bastyr, setting life goals, even leaving behind a previous identity.

-.. .-. . .- --

I was in the fastest swim shape I've ever been in, and arguably in the best overall shape of my life. The momentum was exhilarating. I received an email from Dr. Meng, my research mentor. She had heard from Paul Amieux, who was running the research presentations for the AIHM 2020 annual conference. I've been dreaming of going to this conference for the last two years since I passed out at that AIHM student networking event. The standard ticket price was $250 and I definitely did not have money like that to spend. Dr. Meng told me complimentary tickets were given for Bastyr student researchers. LET'S GOO!! In addition, my work on prostate cancer cells would be showcased at the conference.

"Yesterday was the first week in a while I had any visitors at meditation. My friends Alex and Mica joined in, and I had told them I felt like a puppy dog whose family just came home hahaha. It really was great to see some of my tribe. I miss having the ND student atmosphere around campus. It looks like I might be online through winter quarter as well due to COVID."

Growing up I felt like I was always concerned with being cool enough. I think it's an innate human desire to be wanted, loved, and accepted. Back then it was taking the shape of "being cool." Living a party lifestyle in San Diego, having my own fraternity, and having lit parties at my house made me feel really cool. I felt wanted, loved, and accepted.

As I grew older, I learned that chasing the party non-stop came with a price. Those late nights led to disrespecting the limits of drugs and alcohol. It got me into trouble, put me out of commission, and even held me back from my dreams. Excelling in school, giving speeches, and meditating also gave me a sense of fulfillment. These actions also brought me towards my dreams. I think almost everything in life is a balancing act. Bringing awareness to how the scales are tipping can be invaluable.

Chapter 12:
Pounding Chest

"Don't ask what the world needs, ask what makes you come alive.
Because what the world needs most, is more people who come alive."
-Howard Thurman

Wow. I won the club competition at Willows Voices Toastmasters this morning. It felt like such an honor. I was competing against Xiahua and DJ, both incredible speakers. Xiahua was actually disqualified since she went over time. Both of their speeches literally gave me chills. Such an incredible, polished competition.

Toastmasters has a competition season every year, which starts in February and goes until August/September. There is another level of competition each month. If you win your first competition at your local club, you then move on to a regional competition featuring multiple clubs. If you win that competition, you move onto a bigger region, etc.

Toastmasters is really good at nit-picking your bad habits. I found myself recording, watching, then rehearsing again, trying to minimize things such as licking lips or excessive eye blinking. I got so fired up to see how far I would go in competition. More practice, and more feedback would be my strategy for preparation. I started reaching out to clubs all over the nation to be a guest speaker. Since COVID was in full swing, everyone was gathering on Zoom meetings. I was able to visit clubs in LA, Boston, New York, Chicago, and New Orleans without moving from my workspace at home.

..—. .— —— .. .—.. —.——

I had been contemplating this concept of finite and infinite games. Everyone plays both types of games. Finite games have a measurable objective. Score more points than the opponent. While it is easy to determine a winner, and track your progress, there is also some degree of anxiety around reaching that objective. Additionally, once you reach the end of a finite game, there is a loss of higher purpose.

Infinite games do not have a measurable objective. They are timeless, and it is a pursuit that you can continue to invest in without feeling pressured to meet a measurable goal. Playing a sport purely for the love of the game is an example of an infinite game. Often we are invested in both finite and infinite games. In America, there is a large culture around winning. We love the self-made man, and the sports phenom. Consequently we tend to invest more energy into finite games that define these personas. This can come at a cost of anxiety around reaching those finite goals.

I wanted to try it out in my own life. I was playing water polo on weeknights, and noticed that when I didn't perform well (in terms of stats) I was really hard on myself. Sometimes it would even keep me up at night, or put me in a bad mood for a while. I was getting in the pool to play ball for fun. Or at least, I wanted to.

I tried meditating before practice with the intention of just having fun. I noticed I was still analytical throughout and after the game, but with a lighter heart. The largest difference: it was some of the most fun and the most creative ball I've ever played. I had a great performance, featuring a few no-look shots over Guy's shoulder, a weak side turn to a t-shot (also over his shoulder), and some beautiful outside shots, among a string of assists and steals. My attention continues to turn to the experience of setting intentions and infinite games, and how it really does provide an organic framework for the spirit to nurture and live.

-- · ·- -· ···

Winner of the Division E contest! I couldn't believe it! That means I've won the club, area, and division-level competitions. District 2 competition would be next, which covers almost the entire state of Washington! District 2 hosts a week-long conference, with the competition as the final event. I was super thankful for all the guidance I've received on this path. Toastmasters is really good at providing you with resources to level up.

Public speaking is both a science and an art. There are very specific techniques you can use to more effectively express yourself to the audience. And at the same time, you have to push outside those parameters to do something unique and creative, to craft something beautiful that grabs the audience's attention. Attention is a weird concept. I remember professor McHan saying that the average human attention span is frighteningly short. Something like 8 seconds. Unless you are doing something creative, that is.

When I was preparing for contests, there was a seasoned speaker, Omar Rivas, who asked me:

"What do you want out of this competition? Do you want to deliver your message to inspire your audience, or do you want to win?"

I'm still perplexed by that question. Couldn't you argue that if you do one well you are also doing the other well? I think maybe he was saying that winning is a tier above just delivering your message. Just delivering your message would not be enough to win the competition. Everyone you are up against has a great message that they are delivering. That's how they've gotten this far. Now, you have to get an edge on your competition.

—. ——— —... ——— —.. —.—— ——. . — ...

"Fkn restless rn. I had a great start to the day with a great willows voices meeting. Got in the pool and threw the ball, mostly a productive day. Then I was playing an awful macro game of League. Took it pretty hard, one dude talking shit too that was doing even worse. I'm 24 hours into a fast sitting outside the gym. Thought about grabbing a snack at the gas station 10 times. I don't even have the

energy to lift rn, honestly just wanna go to bed. Tomorrow will be a new day."

District 2 finals went well! I did not place in the top 3, but I was happy with the work and progress I had made in my craft. When I was a kid, we traveled a lot for water polo tournaments. There was a certain magic to traveling out of your hometown into a new place and going head to head with the best competition in the area. The pool deck would be buzzing with the spirit of sport.

Instead of traveling to a new land, I simply hopped into a Zoom black mirror for the speech contest. I felt like something was missing. I hoped events wouldn't stay like this forever.

.-.. . ..-. - -... . ... -. -..

Graduation was kind of weird... How deep had I really developed relationships since COVID took over? I certainly had developed some, but in my class I felt like I didn't know them deeply. We hardly ever hung out outside of class, and didn't talk to each other just to talk. Since half of the program was online, I noticed this chasm of intimacy between people.

Throughout this course of events I started to realize how to actually build strong relationships with people. Go out of your way to talk to them, be involved in their life, and see how they're doing. It sounds so simple when I write it down, but how often does this actually happen for people? Finding really true, deep relationships can be a rarity.

Everyone was emotional at graduation, which was expected. To me, I felt like things weren't over. I knew I had an entire journey that I was barely starting. I didn't feel like much had ended. I've noticed I actually get way more excited about beginning things than I do when I end things. I'm a simp for the infinite game.

When the ceremony was over and we got back to my uncle's house, Dad gave me a letter. He kept making comments like: "we've been waiting to give you this for a long time." What did he mean by that?

There was a note with the letter that read: "To: Armani and Gaetani". He explained that Guy received this exact letter when he graduated. My turn to open the letter had been long waiting. I hadn't put the pieces together until I opened the envelope and read "grandson" on the card. Nonni had given us graduation gifts before she passed away. It was the best cry I've had in a while. I didn't look at the gift amount until later: over 600 in cash. My Dad's sister suggested I use some of the money to buy a keepsake by which I'll remember her. I want to get something that I can remember both Nonno and Nonni by. Something that keeps them close, that reminds me of my roots.

Grandma on my mom's side sent a grad card with cash as well. She gave me a phone call shortly after.

"Don't spend it all on one six-pack!" I had a good laugh. She's a funny one.

--- .-.

The summer of 2021 was filled with hikes, camping, river floats, nights dancing, and massage. The program I took was a summer intensive with Bellevue Massage School. The school had a partnership with Bastyr University. The program entailed transferring the book work, so the summer could be spent learning hands-on. I was getting a 90 minute massage four days a week. Working with the body was inspiring, and I knew this would be a great step into practicing healing before I started grad school.

One weekend I went camping with a bunch of the guys from The Perimeter. We backpacked through the Eastern Sierra Nevada's. It was absolutely gorgeous. One day my brother and his friend, Austin, took a dip in a lake which was quite chilly. They swam the length across, and on the way back Austin started slowing down. He didn't have the water polo experience under his belt. I yelled to my brother that he needed help.

Guy swam back out to Austin just as his strokes became nonexistent (the first major sign that drowning was coming next). Guy had a bit of pool lifeguard experience, and that previous training equipped him well to bring Austin back to shore safely. Our group was relieved, and celebrated the teamwork and support that was displayed. The best part: both Guy and Austin were butt-naked.

Backpacking through the Eastern Sierra Nevada's

My brother asked me one day while we were camping: If I had a Native American name, what would it be? I thought about it for maybe two seconds.

"Pounding Chest."

"Pounding Chest. Oooh, that's a good one. Why Pounding Chest?"

"I've always physically had a big chest, and I like to pound it. I also find myself charging challenges no matter how tough my circumstances might be."

··-· --- ·-· --· --- - - · -·

"Everything starts with a sensory input. Our environment plays a significant role in who we become. We are able to filter our sensory inputs, but the input must be there to produce any thought or action whatsoever. How can we cultivate the most ideal environment then? How can we evaluate the environments we are currently in and then optimize and alter them for the desired result? Being bored at home is a state that is produced by a sensory input. The thought and therefore action of playing a video game begins with a sensory input and is then magnified through the filter of past experience and habit to be manifested in full strength. This environment can be altered to reduce the sensory input and then change the course of action. What other filters might be necessary to produce a given effect? Maybe listening to more podcasts on the harm of video games. Maybe more meditation. How can I create an environment where I meditate more consistently? Well, an environment with a cushion, a quiet place, and a place without distractions is really ideal."

After graduation I moved to Portland, Oregon for chiropractic school. I got an amazing job at Valleyview Injury + Physical Medicine as a Licensed Massage Therapist. Valleyview was a large natural-health focused clinic near Portland that offered chiropractic care, massage therapy, physical therapy, acupuncture, and injection therapy. The environment I found myself in felt incredibly aligned with the work I wanted to do. I also had some amazing people around me that were encouraging and serious about their work. They also knew how to have a good time and share some great laughs.

I found myself rejoicing in my freedom. Any day not imprisoned between four walls was a great day.

When I drove to work on a sunny day and saw Mt. Hood in all her glory, I hooted, hollered, and pounded my chest as I took in the beauty, strength, and tenacity of our Earth. The sun and mountain imbued my spirit with focused ambition for the day.

When I drove to work on a cloudy day I looked in awe at the Columbia River Gorge, and the iconic misty forests of the pacific northwest. It relaxed me in a subtle way, and instilled my spirit with patient curiosity for the day.

These effects are both subtle and profound. The more you look for them, and believe in them, the more you can draw on the power of your environment to help you manifest your optimized evolution.

"No matter how broken your past, or destructive your habits might be, you can always choose to reinvent the story, and there are forces around you that will help you do so."

Life goals update:

Goals

He is versed in 3 varieties of ancient medicine - (Ayurveda, Hippocrates, TCM, Egyptian)
He can speak a native language in 3 continents of the world
He has clogged a toilet in 10 countries *5/10*
He once helped a family in need in a developing country
He transcended a sea with the wind
Both his publications have helped propel the field of medicine
With one speech, he reaches 1,000 ears *~300/1000*
His guitar sings to him
Life wrote his autobiography **volume 1**
~~He once refused to eat food for 10 days~~
He loves to dance, on his hands
He climbed 3 mountains *1/3*
He performs a split... without using a banana
He is the life of parties he's never attended
The soil thanks his garden for its presence (more than 10 plants)
He falls upwards
Salmon rejoice when they find his spear
He once parallel parked a train
He once took an astronaut flying
Meditation asked him for awareness on its retreat
His piss pisses on Niagara Falls
He once surfed a wave 4 times taller than he is
~~His greatest achievement is changing one person's life in a small way~~ *infinite game :)*

I don't always drink wine, but when I do, I prefer my own.
He is...

Complete 5 by age 30 *2/5*
5 more by 35
5 more by 40
5 more by 50

Additions:

Conferences rejoice at his tongue
His scholarship foundation funded students 200 years from
today
He does more pullups than his 20 year old grandchildren
His dog performs a backflip on command
He founded a health center with experts in medicine from
different corners of the globe

Acknowledgements

I want to first thank Lily for helping me make sense of my words when I felt like a toddler. Your selfless generosity is deeply appreciated.

Thank you to Dustin, B3ntl3y, and Richard for helping me out with photography and graphic design. Your individual expertise supported me immensely in foreign territory.

Thank you to Mom for giving me my first journal that I carried with me to class in second grade. The practice of journaling has been immeasurably valuable for me, and this book would not have happened without it.

Thank you to all my friends and family that provided unconditional support. Even the smallest ounce of enthusiasm or recognition provided the juice to keep me going on the tough writing days.

Bio:

Armani Antonellis lives in Portland, Oregon and works as a Licensed Massage Therapist in an integrative clinic. He enjoys living life on the edge, pursuing supernatural potential, and dancing with his demons. In his free time, he writes, reads, lifts, plays water polo, takes psychedelic walks through the forest, and bathes in electronic music. Armani loves connecting and collaborating. If any readers would like to connect, share their goals list, or chat about the meaning of life please don't hesitate to reach out at poundingmychest@gmail.com

Highly recommended readings from the author

Grain Brain - David Perlmutter
Own the Day, Own Your Life - Aubrey Marcus
Think and Grow Rich - Napoleon Hill
The Genius Myth - Michael Meade
Can't Hurt Me - David Goggins
The Rational Male - Rollo Tomassi
48 Laws of Power - Robert Greene
King, Warrior, Magician, Lover: Rediscovering the Archetypes
    of the Mature Masculine - Douglas Gillette and Robert L.
    Moore
You Are the Placebo - Joe Dispenza
The Biology of Belief - Bruce Lipton
Living with a SEAL - Jesse Itzler

The encoded message in chapter 1 is a quote belonging to Renes Descartes, and the coded messages in chapters 7 and 12 belong to Lilo from "Lilo and Stitch"